BY THE SAME AUTHOR
Marxism and Christianity
After Virtue
Whose Justice? Which Rationality?
Three Rival Versions of Moral Enquiry

Dependent
Rational
Animals

Dependent Rational Animals

Why Human Beings Need the Virtues

ALASDAIR MACINTYRE

Duckworth

This edition 2009
First published in 1999 by
Gerald Duckworth & Co. Ltd.
90-93 Cowcross Street, London EC1M 6BF
Tel: 020 7490 7300
Fax: 020 7490 0080
inquiries@duckworth-publishers.co.uk
www.ducknet.co.uk

Published by arrangement with Open Court Publishing Company,
A division of Carus Publishing Company, 315 Fifth Street,
P.O.Box 300, Peru, Illinois 61354, USA

A catalogue record for this book is available
from the British Library

ISBN 978 0 7156 3860 6

1006561806

Printed and bound in Great Britain by
CPI Antony Rowe, Chippenham and Eastbourne

Contents

Preface

It was in 1925 that John Dewey delivered the first series of Paul Carus Lectures, newly endowed by members of the Carus family, and shortly afterwards published by the Open Court Publishing Company as *Experience and Nature*. The Lectures were and are a memorial to Dr. Paul Carus, graduate of Tübingen, founder of the *Open Court* and the *Monist*, and Director of the Open Court Publishing Company until his death in 1919. And for more than seventy years the American philosophical community has had reason for continuing gratitude to Dr. Carus himself, to the Carus family and to the Open Court Publishing Company. To which I now add my own.

This book is a revised and expanded version of three Carus Lectures delivered at the Pacific Division meetings of the American Philosophical Association in 1997. The task of rewriting has made me aware of how much more needed to be said than was then said. And now rereading the written version has made me even more aware of the inadequacies of my answers to the two main questions that I have addressed. But about the central importance of these questions, not only for philosophers in their professional enquiries, but also for everyone engaged in reflection on the moral dimensions of their practice, I am more strongly convinced than I was at the outset.

Both questions—'Why is it important for us to attend to and to understand what human beings have in common with members of other intelligent animal species?' and 'What makes attention to human vulnerability and disability important for moral philosophers?'—and especially the second have so far received insufficient attention within moral philosophy. It may therefore seem that I am engaged in a work of correction and so I am. But the philosopher whose failure to recognize the importance of these questions and whose consequent errors and limitations I am chiefly anxious to correct is myself. So that this book is not only a continuation of, but also a correction of some of my earlier enquiries in *After Virtue, Whose Justice? Which Rationality?* and *Three Rival Versions of Moral Enquiry*.

In *After Virtue* I had attempted to give an account of the place of the virtues, understood as Aristotle had understood them, within social practices, the lives of individuals and the lives of communities, while making that account independent of what I called Aristotle's "metaphysical biology." Although there is indeed good reason to repudiate important elements in Aristotle's biology, I now judge that I was in error in supposing an ethics independent of biology to be possible—and I am grateful to those critics who argued this case against me—and this for two distinct, but related reasons. The first is that no account of the goods, rules and virtues that are definitive of our moral life can be adequate that does not explain—or at least point us towards an explanation—how that form of life is possible for beings who are biologically constituted as we are, by providing us with an account of our development towards and into that form of life. That development has as its starting point our initial animal condition. Secondly, a failure to understand that condition and the light thrown upon it by a comparison between humans and members of other intelligent animal species will obscure crucial features of that development. One such failure, of immense importance on its own account, is the nature and extent of human vulnerability and disability. And by not reckoning adequately with this central feature of human life I had necessarily failed to notice some other important aspects of the part that the virtues play in human life.

A second area in which I need to correct as well as to develop what I have written earlier concerns the relationship of Aristotle to Aquinas, as I had characterized it in *Whose Justice? Which*

Rationality? and in *Three Rival Versions of Moral Enquiry*. I remain in general convinced by those commentators who have stressed the extent to which Aquinas in his philosophical enquiries was not just an Aristotelian, but often a keenly perceptive interpreter as well as adapter of Aristotle. But I had been misled, in part by Aquinas's use of something like Davidson's principle of charity in his interpretation of Aristotle, into underestimating the degree and the importance of the differences in their attitudes to the acknowledgment of dependence. I was first struck by this when reading a prayer composed by Aquinas in which he asks God to grant that he may happily share with those in need what he has, while humbly asking for what he needs from those who have, a prayer that in effect, although not by Aquinas's own intention, asks that we may not share some of the attitudes of Aristotle's *megalopsychos*. This led me to reflect upon how Aquinas's account of the virtues not only supplements, but also corrects Aristotle's to a significantly greater extent than I had realized. But this affected a good deal more than my reading of parts of Aquinas's moral philosophy.

It had not been to philosophy that I owed my own first realization of the parts played in human life by vulnerability to physical and mental dangers and harms. And I took longer than I should have done to arrive at an understanding of the importance of the absence of that realization from the greater part of moral philosophy. Rereading Aquinas not only underlined that importance, but directed me towards resources that he provides for an account of the virtues that reckoned not only with our animal condition, but also with the need to acknowledge our consequent vulnerability and dependence.

Just because my account of the virtues is that of a Thomistic Aristotelian, it is in varying degrees at odds not only with the views of other types of Aristotelian, but also with those advanced by Kantians, utilitarians and contractarians. There are passages in this book where I have taken note of some of these disagreements, but this has been primarily for the purpose of clarifying the account that I am defending. No one who holds one of these conflicting views should suppose that I believe that I have provided anything remotely approaching a refutation of their views. What I have issued is rather an invitation: to show how from each of their standpoints due place can be given to the facts about animality, disability and vulnerability and the need to acknowledge these.

There is of course a good deal of unfinished philosophical business in these pages. I have presupposed the truth of certain philosophical positions, the defense of which requires extended argument, and I have done no more than gesture in the direction of that argument. Four areas especially should be noticed: human identity, perception, the relationship of evaluative judgment to factual judgment, and the psychological reality of certain types of character trait. For the positions that I have taken involve a rejection of Lockean accounts of personal identity, of Kantian or quasiKantian views of perception, of a number of standpoints in metaethics, and of skepticism about the psychological reality of character traits, and therefore about the reality of virtues and vices. But, since each of these requires treatment at considerable length, I have not been able to supply it here.

Finally let me with warmest gratitude catalogue my numerous particular debts: to my father who long ago made me aware of these issues; to those whose writings more recently reinforced that awareness, especially in their different ways Eva Feder Kittay, Hans S. Reinders, Anita Silvers, and Thomas I. White; next to those who read part or all of this book at various stages in its preparation, who rescued me from a variety of errors, and whose verdict on this final version will in some cases at least be that I did not learn nearly enough from them: Robert Brandon, Owen Flanagan, Eugene Garver, Eva Feder Kittay, Robert B. Louden, John McDowell, Janet Mann, Anita Silvers, David Solomon, Thomas I. White, the late Margaret D. Wilson, and those members of the department of philosophy at Boston College, Georgetown University and the University of Notre Dame who discussed earlier versions of parts of the text; and to

Larry D. Russell for the major part that he played in the production of this book. My greatest indebtedness is to my wife, Lynn Sumida Joy, to my daughters, Toni, Jean and Helen, and to my son, Daniel.

Alasdair MacIntyre

Durham, North Carolina
October, 1998

1

Vulnerability, dependence, animality

We human beings are vulnerable to many kinds of affliction and most of us are at some time afflicted by serious ills. How we cope is only in small part up to us. It is most often to others that we owe our survival, let alone our flourishing, as we encounter bodily illness and injury, inadequate nutrition, mental defect and disturbance, and human aggression and neglect. This dependence on particular others for protection and sustenance is most obvious in early childhood and in old age. But between these first and last stages our lives are characteristically marked by longer or shorter periods of injury, illness or other disablement and some among us are disabled for their entire lives.

These two related sets of facts, those concerning our vulnerabilities and afflictions and those concerning the extent of our dependence on particular others are so evidently of singular importance that it might seem that no account of the human condition whose authors hoped to achieve credibility could avoid giving them a central place. Yet the history of Western moral philosophy suggests otherwise. From Plato to Moore and since there are usually, with some rare exceptions, only passing references to human vulnerability and affliction and to the connections between them and our dependence on others. Some of the facts of human limitation and of our consequent need of cooperation with others are more generally acknowledged, but for the most part only then to be put on one side.

And when the ill, the injured and the otherwise disabled *are* presented in the pages of moral philosophy books, it is almost always exclusively as possible subjects of benevolence by moral agents who are themselves presented as though they were continuously rational, healthy and untroubled. So we are invited, when we do think of disability, to think of "the disabled" as "them," as other than "us," as a separate class, not as ourselves as we have been, sometimes are now and may well be in the future.

Adam Smith provides us with an example. While discussing what it is that makes the "pleasures of wealth and greatness . . . strike the imagination as something grand and beautiful," he remarks that "in the languor of disease and the weariness of old age" we cease to be so impressed, for we then take note of the fact that the acquisition of wealth and greatness leaves their possessors "always as much, and sometimes more exposed than before, to anxiety, to fear and to sorrow, to diseases, to danger, and to death" (*The Theory of Moral Sentiments* IV, chapter I). But to allow our attention to dwell on this is, on Smith's view, misguided.

To do so is to embrace a "splenetic philosophy," the effect of "sickness or low spirits" upon an imagination "which in pain and sorrow seems to be confined," so that we are no longer "charmed with the beauty of that accommodation which reigns in the palaces and economy of the great . . . ." The imagination of those "in better health or in better humor" fosters what may, Smith concedes, be no more than seductive illusions about the pleasures of wealth and greatness, but they are economically beneficial illusions. "It is this deception which rouses and keeps in continual motion the industry of mankind." So even someone as perceptive as Smith, when he does pause to recognize the perspectives of ill health and old age, finds reason at once to put them on one side. And in so doing Smith speaks for moral philosophy in general.

As with vulnerability and affliction, so it is correspondingly with dependence. Dependence on others is of course often recognized in a general way, usually as something that we need in order to achieve our positive goals. But an acknowledgment of anything like the full extent of that dependence and of the ways in which it stems from our vulnerability and our afflictions is generally absent. Feminist philosophers have recently done something to remedy this, not only by their understanding of the connections between blindness to and denigration of women and male attempts to ignore the facts of dependence, but also—I think here particularly of the work of Virginia Held—by their emphasis upon the importance of the mother-child relationship as a paradigm for moral relationships. Even more recently some striking philosophical work has been done on the nature of disability and on the condition of the disabled and the dependent, for example, in the Netherlands by Hans S. Reinders and in the United States by Eva Feder Kittay, who has also been an important contributor to feminist discussions (see Hans S. Reinders' work in progress, *Should We Prevent Handicapped Lives? Reflections on the Future of Disabled People in Liberal Society,* and Eva Feder Kittay, 'Human Dependency and Rawlsian Equality' in *Feminists Rethink the Self*, ed. Diana Tietjens Meyers, Boulder, Colorado: Westview Press, 1996; 'Taking Dependency Seriously: The Family and Medical Leave Act Considered in Light of the Social Organization of Dependency Work and Gender Equality', *Hypatia* 10, 1, Winter 1995; and '"Not *My* Way, Sesha, *Your* Way, Slowly"': "Maternal Thinking" in the Raising of a Child with Profound Intellectual Disabilities' in *No Easy Answers: Mothering in the US Today*, ed. Julia Hanisberg and Sara Ruddick, New York: Beacon Press, 1998. Her forthcoming book, *Love's Labor: Essays on Equality, Dependence and Care*, London & New York: Routledge, 1999, will be an important focus for future discussion. See also Susan Wendell, *The Rejected Body: Feminist Philosophical Reflections on Disability*, New York: Routledge, 1996, and the review of it by Anita Silvers in *Ethics* 108, 3, April, 1998. Another landmark book will be *Disability, Difference, Discrimination: Perspectives on Justice in Bioethics and Public Policy* by Anita Silvers, David Wasserman, and Mary Mahowald, with an Afterword by Lawrence Becker, Lanham, MD: Rowman and Littlefield, 1999.).

But such work is only beginning to make any systematic impact on what is currently established as mainstream moral philosophy in the advanced societies of the West. And, given those characteristics of the Western inheritance in moral philosophy that I have just noted, this is scarcely surprising.

The question therefore arises: what difference to moral philosophy would it make, if we were to treat the facts of vulnerability and affliction and the related facts of dependence as central to the human condition? As does the further question: how should we begin to try to answer this question? In philosophy where one begins generally makes a difference to the outcome of one's enquiries. One possible starting point is to acknowledge that the habits of mind that have been apt to obscure the significance of the facts of affliction and dependence for the moral philosopher are not only widely shared, but genuinely difficult to discard. They are after all *our* habits, part of a mindset that many of us have acquired, not only from our engagement in the enquiries of moral philosophy, but from the wider culture which provides the background of those enquiries. So we might do well to begin with a certain suspicion of ourselves. For whatever the philosophical idiom in which we frame our initial enquiries, whatever the philosophical resources upon which we find ourselves able to draw, we will be liable to think in terms that may prevent us from understanding just how much of a change in standpoint is needed.

Consider how both physical and mental disability are afflictions of the body and how therefore habits of mind that express an attitude of denial towards the facts of disability and dependence presuppose either a failure or a refusal to acknowledge adequately the bodily dimensions of our existence. This failure or refusal is perhaps rooted in, is certainly reinforced by the extent to which we conceive of ourselves and imagine ourselves as other than animal, as exempt from the hazardous condition of "mere" animality. Such defective modes of self-understanding and imagination at the level of everyday thought and practice seem often to coexist without any notable difficulty with a theoretical acknowledgment of the past evolutionary history of human beings. But cultural prejudice often divorces the human present from the human past. And this same cultural prejudice sometimes finds support in philosophical theorizing that is itself innocent of prejudice. So philosophical theories about what it is that distinguishes members of our species from other animal species—it has been alleged by some theorists, as we shall see, that nonhuman animals cannot have thoughts, beliefs or reasons for action—may seem to provide grounds for the belief that our rationality as thinking beings is somehow independent of our animality. We become in consequence forgetful of our bodies and of how our thinking is the thinking of one species of animal.

There is also another and perhaps more fundamental relationship between our animal condition and our vulnerabilities. It will be a central thesis of this book that the virtues that we need, if we are to develop from our initial animal condition into that of independent rational agents, and the virtues that we need, if we are to confront and respond to vulnerability and disability both in ourselves and in others, belong to one and the same set of virtues, the distinctive virtues of dependent rational animals, whose dependence, rationality and animality have to be understood in relationship to each other.

If therefore we are to reckon adequately with the facts of disability and dependence, it may perhaps be to the point to begin with and from a reassertion of human animality. One way to do this is to return to Aristotle's texts, if only because no philosopher has taken human animality more seriously. Yet even the relevant texts of Aristotle can be and sometimes have been read in a way that deprives them of their instructive power. All nonhuman animals, Aristotle wrote, "live by perceptions and memories and have little experience; but the human kind live also by art and reasonings" (*Metaphysics* A, 980b 25–28). And Aristotle's account of human beings as distinctively rational has sometimes been interpreted as though he meant that rationality was not itself an animal property, but rather a property that separates humans from their animality. Aristotle did not of course make this mistake. *Phronesis*, the capacity for practical rationality (*Nicomachean Ethics* VI 1140b 4–6, 20–21) is a capacity that he—and after him Aquinas—ascribed to some nonhuman animals in virtue of their foresight (1141a 26–28), as well as to human beings. This of course does raise the question of how the *phronesis* of some types of nonhuman animal is related to specifically and distinctively human rationality. But some commentators have ignored this problem and in so doing have failed to ask the relevant questions about the relationship between our rationality and our animality. They have underestimated the importance of the fact that our bodies are animal bodies with the identity and continuities of animal bodies, and they have failed to recognize adequately that in this present life it is true of us that we do not merely have, but are our bodies. Other commentators have understood this. And it was his reading not only of Aristotle, but also of Ibn Rushd's commentary that led Aquinas to assert: "Since the soul is part of the body of a human being, the soul is not the whole human being and my soul is not I" (*Commentary on Paul's First Letter to the Corinthians* XV, 1, 11; note also that Aquinas, unlike most moderns, often refers to nonhuman animals as "other animals"). This is a lesson that those of us who identify ourselves as contemporary Aristotelians may need to relearn, perhaps from those phenomenological investigations that enabled Merleau-Ponty also to conclude that I am my body.

Forgetfulness of human animality is of course not the only obstacle to acknowledging the facts of affliction and dependence. And Aristotle himself exemplifies two other attitudes that are barriers to this acknowledgment. For while Aristotle understood very well the importance of the relevant kinds of experience for rational practice—"we see," he wrote, "that the experienced are more effective than those who have reason, but lack experience" (*Metaphysics* A 981a 14–15) — in neither ethics nor politics did he give any weight to the experience of those for whom the facts of affliction and dependence are most likely to be undeniable: women, slaves, and servants, those engaged in the productive labor of farmers, fishing crews, and manufacture. "On important matters we undertake deliberation in common with others, distrusting ourselves as inadequate to make decisions" (*Nicomachean Ethics* III 1112b 10–11). But it matters a good deal with which others we choose to deliberate and Aristotle's own failure to acknowledge the facts of affliction and dependence may be in part at least a consequence of his political exclusions.

Another Aristotelian obstacle to that acknowledgment is constituted by two characteristics of Aristotle's conception of masculine virtue. When Aristotle discusses the particular need that we have for friends in times of adversity and loss, he insists that men who are manly differ from women in being unwilling to have others saddened by their grief. They do not want, by sharing their loss, to inflict it on others (*Nicomachean Ethics* IX 1171b 6012). And Aristotle plainly takes it that the man who acts like a woman in this regard is inferior in his masculine virtue. Moreover, the magnanimous man, who is on Aristotle's account, a paragon of the virtues, dislikes any recognition of his need for aid from and consolation by others. He "is ashamed to receive benefits, because it is a mark of a superior to confer benefits, of an inferior to receive them" (*Nicomachean Ethics* IV 1124b 9–10). And Aristotle goes on to remark that the magnanimous man is forgetful of what he has received, but remembers what he has given, and is not pleased to be reminded of the former, but hears the latter recalled with pleasure" (12–18).

Aristotle thus anticipated Smith—and a great many others—in importing into moral philosophy the standpoint of those who have taken themselves to be self-sufficiently superior and of those who take their standards from those who take themselves to be self-sufficiently superior. And he also and correspondingly anticipated them in being unable to give due recognition to affliction and to dependence. Nonetheless when we try to remedy this injury to moral philosophy, it will turn out, so I shall be suggesting, that we have to draw to a quite remarkable extent upon Aristotle's concepts, theses and arguments. Even although Aristotle and some Aristotelians have positions against which it is important to argue, it was Aristotle who provided the best resources that we as yet have for identifying what is mistaken in those positions and how those mistakes should be corrected. So at certain points I will be turning Aristotle against Aristotle, sometimes with the aid of Aquinas, and this in the interests of defending three sets of theses.

The first concerns our resemblances to and commonality with members of some other intelligent animal species. I shall contend that, although our differences from all other species are certainly of crucial importance, it is also important that both initially in our earliest childhood activities and to some significant extent thereafter we comport ourselves towards the world in much the same way as other intelligent animals. In transcending some of their limitations we never separate ourselves entirely from what we share with them. Indeed our ability to transcend those limitations depends in part upon certain of those animal characteristics, among them the nature of our identity.

It is not just that our bodies are animal bodies with the identity and the continuities of animal bodies, as I have already asserted. Human identity is primarily, even if not only, bodily and therefore animal identity and it is by reference to that identity that the continuities of our relationships to others are partly defined. Among the various ills that afflict us are those that disturb those continuities—loss of or damage to memory, for example, or disfigurement that prevents others from recognizing us—as well as those that disable us in other ways.

A second set of theses concerns the moral importance of acknowledging not only such vulnerabilities and afflictions, but also our consequent dependences. Modern moral philosophy has understandably and rightly placed great emphasis upon individual autonomy, upon the capacity for making independent choices. I shall argue that the virtues of independent rational agency need for their adequate exercise to be accompanied by what I shall call the virtues of acknowledged dependence and that a failure to understand this is apt to obscure some features of rational agency. Moreover both sets of virtues are needed in order to actualize the distinctive potentialities that are specific to the human rational animal. Identifying how and why they are needed is a prerequisite for understanding their essential place in the kind of human life through which human flourishing can be achieved.

What type of social relationship and what type of conception of the common good are required, if a social group is to be one in and through which both the virtues of rational independence and the virtues of acknowledged dependence are sustained and transmitted? A third set of theses provides answers to those questions and I shall argue that neither the modern nation-state nor the modern family can supply the kind of political and social association that is needed.

2

Humans as contrasted with, humans as included in the class of animals

Animals come when their names are called. Just like human beings.
—L. Wittgenstein

From its earliest sixteenth-century uses in English and other European languages 'animal' and whatever other expressions correspond to it have been employed both to name a class whose members include spiders, bees, chimpanzees, dolphins *and* humans—among others, but not plants, inanimate beings, angels and God, and also to name the class consisting only of nonhuman animals. It is this latter use that became dominant in modern Western cultures and with it a habit of mind that, by distracting our attention from how much we share with certain other animal species, puts itself at odds both with older Aristotelian modes of thought and with modern postDarwinian evolutionary naturalism. Aristotelians had focused attention on the distinction between the living and the inanimate, including human beings under the genus 'animal' so that even the specific rationality of human beings is to be understood as animal rationality. And from Darwin we should by now have learned that human history, whatever else it is, is the natural history of one more animal species and that to understand such a history comparison with the history of certain other animal species may always be and often is necessary (for discussions of the relationship of Aristotle to Darwin see E. Gilson, *From Aristotle to Darwin and Back Again*, tr. J. Lyon, Notre Dame: University of Notre Dame Press, 1984, and especially Larry Arnhart, *Darwinian Natural Right: The Biological Ethics of Human Nature*, Albany, NY: State University of New York Press, 1998).

We all of us, or almost all of us, know this. But there are too many contexts in which we allow ourselves to forget it, a cultural tendency that is reinforced by too exclusive an attention to and exaggeration of what does indeed distinguish human beings from members of all other species. Among these reinforcements is that of a certain kind of recent philosophy, a reinforcement all the more powerful because of that philosophy's extraordinary achievements in enquiring into the nature of language and the range of ways in which the use of language enables us to relate to those to whom and that about which we speak. Those enquiries have had a central place, often *the* central place, both for those philosophers for whom the names to reckon with have been those of Wittgenstein, Austin, Quine, and Davidson and for those for whom Husserl, Heidegger and Gadamer have been the defining influences. The very same patterns of argument with respect to nonhuman animals appear in the writings of both.

Commonly the arguments run something like this. Some particular human capacity is made the object of enquiry: the capacity for having thoughts, or beliefs, or the ability to act for reasons, or the power to frame and use concepts. And it is then shown how, contrary to the views of some philosophical predecessor, the human exercise of this particular capacity involves the possession and use of language. It is finally further concluded that, because nonhuman animals do not possess language, or at least the requisite kind of language, they must also lack the capacity or ability or power in question. So it has been argued variously that nonhuman animals cannot have thoughts, must lack beliefs, cannot act for reasons and in their

encounters with the objects of their experience must be innocent of concepts.

Philosophers who arrive at these negative conclusions are
generally careful not to deny that nonhuman animals perceive,
feel and in some cases give evidence of at least some intelligence. The silliness of Descartes's insistence that nonhuman
animals not only lack thoughts and intelligence, but also
genuine perceptions and feelings has provided a salutary warn-
ing. But equally generally—there are rare and important
exceptions—such philosophers seldom entertain the thought
that the resemblances and analogies between the perceptions,
feelings, and intelligent activities of certain species of nonhuman animal might warrant, not only philosophical attention for
their own sake, but also philosophical attention for the sake of a
more adequate understanding of human perception, feeling,
and practical intelligence. And one reason for this may be the
way in which their conclusions lead them to draw a single line
between all nonhuman animals on the one hand and humans
on the other, so that no attention is paid to particular species of
nonhuman animals whose characteristics might have a peculiar
relevance.

It is not of course that such philosophers do not sometimes
refer to members of particular species as examples. Heidegger's
lizard, Malcolm's dog and cat, Kenny's dog are characteristic
denizens of the literature (Descartes drew examples from sheep
and wolves and from goats, caterpillars and worms.). But the
kind of extended philosophical attention that Jonathan Bennett
(*Rationality*, London: Routledge & Kegan Paul, 1964, pp.
8–32) gave to what is known about bees or that Thomas I.
White ('Is a Dolphin a Person?' in *Discovering Philosophy*, Upper
Saddle River: Prentice Hall, 1996, and, together with Denise L.
Herzing of the Wild Dolphin Project, 'Dolphins and the
Question of Personhood', forthcoming in *Etica & Animali*,
special issue on animals and personhood, 1998) has more
recently given to what has been learned about dolphins is
exceptional. And this matters not only because there are

significant and relevant differences between species. It also matters because the degree of abstraction and distancing involved removes us too far from that direct acquaintance with particular members of particular species from which in the end all our interpretative understanding of animals, human or otherwise, derives. Descartes's misunderstandings were as much about humans as about nonhuman animals. What misled Descartes was his view that our beliefs about the thoughts, feelings and decisions of others are wholly founded on inferences from their overt behavior and utterances. It is of course true that on occasion we do have to 'work out' by inference what someone else must be thinking or feeling. But even in these special types of case we are still relying on a primary and more fundamental interpretative knowledge of the thoughts and feelings of others which does not have and does not need inferential justification. What kind of knowledge is this? It is a form of practical knowledge, a knowing how to interpret, that arises from those complex social interactions with others in which our responses to others and their responses to our responses generate a recognition by them and by us of what thoughts and feelings it is to which each is responding. Of course both they and we sometimes make mistakes, some of us more often than others, but the ability to identify such mistakes itself presupposes an ability to be aware of what others think and feel. Interpretative knowledge of others derives from and is inseparable from involvement with others and the possibility of Cartesian doubt about the thoughts and feelings of others can arise only for those deprived of such involvement either by some grave psychological defect, or, as in the case of Descartes, by the power of some philosophical theory.

Knowledge of others, that is, is a matter of responsive sympathy and empathy elicited through action and interaction and without these we could not, as we often do, impute to those others the kind of reasons for their actions that, by making their actions intelligible to us, enable us to respond to them in ways that they too can find intelligible. (Sometimes of course we respond and have no difficulty in responding to an action, even although we are quite unaware of the reasons, if any, for which it was done. But often it is just because an action was done for this reason rather than that that we respond as we do and only because we are able to identify the reason that we know how to respond.)

In the case of the relationship of human being to human being none of this is, or should be, controversial. But, I want to suggest, there is no significant difference in the case of the relationship of human beings to members of certain other animal species. Consider first how generally and characteristically we develop our ability to tell when certain other humans are in pain. A child, not yet able to speak, falls, bruises herself, and screams. The mother says "Does it hurt?" and puts on a bandage. Presently the child learns in such situations sometimes to replace the scream or the groan by saying 'It hurts' and also to recognize that others have recognized what this utterance expresses, when they say of her 'She is in pain'. Some children, having learned that this is a way of getting adult attention, then say 'It hurts' or 'I am in pain', when this is not true. Mothers and other adults usually know how to detect such lies and to respond appropriately, although sometimes they may be deceived. And here inference does of course find a genuine, even if secondary place. "Don't make such a fuss. Such a mild bruise cannot hurt *that* much."

In this sequence what begins as a set of interactive responses then becomes first a set of recognitions of the intentions embodied in these responses and then a set of recognitions that each of the intentions includes the intention that it should be recognized by the other as the intention that it is. It is to these prelinguistic recognitions that the utterance of such sentences as 'She is in pain' or 'She is concerned that I am in pain' afford expression. And our ability to use and to understand the utterance of such sentences depends upon our having the relevant set of responses and recognitions. The word 'response' and the word 'recognition' are of course no more than useful shorthand for a wide range of types of reactive movement and of types of identification, reidentification, and classification, both informed by directed perceptual attention. But for the moment what matters is only to notice that it is only insofar as and because we participated in some range of such responses and recognitions that we are able to identify what others are thinking and feeling, including their thoughts and feelings about our thoughts and feelings.

It is no different in these respects with our identification of the thoughts and feelings of members of some other animal species. Vicki Hearne has given us an account that is both first-hand and first-rate of what is involved in the relationship of mutual understanding that develops between a human trainer and a dog ('How to Say "Fetch!"',' *Raritan* III, 2, Fall, 1983: 1–33, reprinted as chapter III of *Adam's Task*, New York: Vintage Books, 1987). There is a first stage in which the trainer corrects the dog's spontaneous activity, so that the dog comes to respond to the trainer's corrections and becomes willing to follow the trainer's lead. In a second stage the dog comes to recognize the trainer's intentions, both in doing such things as moving the line on the training-collar, but also in saying 'Sit!' or 'Stand!' The dog now attends to the trainer's intentions and the trainer recognizes the dog's intentions in responding in one way rather than another. So the dog not only learns to respond to 'Sit!' but learns what the trainer intends in saying 'Sit!'

"It turns out that saying 'sit' requires a lot of work on various cases . . . . She'll sit in the middle of the yard, but she won't sit a foot from the fence . . . Sitting when she's calm is not sitting when another dog is inviting her to play . . . I make her sit in as many different situations as ingenuity and luck will provide" (p. 16). But that does not as yet include every type of sitting: "sitting in a puddle of water is deeply unacceptable." The dog's grasp of what falls under the concept 'sit' has been extended until it reaches a limit.

At a third stage the dog by introducing changes into its routines communicates intentions of its own. It clowns or it expresses uneasiness. And even well-trained dogs will be apt to express uneasiness when approached by those who are frightened of dogs because they do not know how to respond to, let alone communicate with them. They are those whom Hearne calls "natural bitees." "Natural bitees are people whose approaches to dogs . . . are contaminated by epistemology" (p. 17). They are those who hope to find premises from which they can infer how the dog will behave, to predict whether it will be apt to bite them or not. Contamination by epistemology prevents those affected—infected? — by it from entering into the only kinds of relationship with dogs, or with members of certain other species, through which interpretative knowledge of their thoughts and feelings can be gained, relationships expressed in responsive activity. And what we acquire from responsive interaction, whether with small human children, or with dogs, or with chimpanzees or gorillas, or with elephants or with dolphins are grounds for approaching with suspicion a certain kind of philosophical theorizing about animals.

To this there will be at least two kinds of response. The first will be to suggest that what Hearne reports about her understanding of dogs and what I claim about human infants are themselves both quite as much informed by—"contaminated by"—philosophical theorizing as are the attitudes that she criticizes. Hearne may have learned from a long line of trainers, from Xenophon to William Koehler, but she reports what she has learned about dogs in terms that show her indebtedness to Wittgenstein—indeed she finds application for the notion of a language-game in the practices of training. And my account of how small children learn the language of pain derives all too plainly from what Wittgenstein says (especially *Philosophical Investigations*, 244) and from thoughts suggested by Paul Grice's theory of the genesis of meaning. But to this it can be said that in neither case does the philosophy provide *grounds* for the relevant assertions. What philosophy has provided is no more than a way of characterizing the kinds of interactive interpretative experience without which we would be unable to ascribe thoughts and feelings to others, whether human infants or dogs or whatever. The interpretative experiences are not of course the same in the two cases; indeed part of the point of the appeal to experience is to remind us that the interpretative experiences through which we acquire this ability are in significant measure species-specific.

To this the reply may well be that, although accounts of interpretative practice and experience, such as Hearne's, may instruct us about how we do in fact come to ascribe thoughts, feelings and intentions to some types of nonhuman animal, they are irrelevant in answering the question of what kinds of ascription of thought, feeling and intention it is that we are *entitled* to make. It is here, so it will be said, that only philosophical enquiry and argument can adjudicate. What only philosophy can determine are the limits of application for such concepts as those of a belief, of a thought, of a reason for action, and of an ability to possess and find application for concepts. And with this we need to quarrel—and our quarrel will itself be a philosophical quarrel—only if it implies a denial that philosophical arguments in this area sometimes stand in need of correction from the standpoint of practice and experience. When philosophers have said "It must be so" and those with the relevant kind of experience say "It is not so," the philosophers have not always been in the right. How then should we proceed?

My overall argument will develop in three parts. First I will recount some of the observed facts about members of one particular intelligent nonhuman species that have seemed to many, although not to all, of those who have interacted with them to justify the ascription of beliefs, thoughts, feelings, reasons for action, and concept acquisition and possession. Secondly I will set out the philosophical arguments whose conclusion is either that some subset of these ascriptions cannot be justified or that no such ascription can be justified. And finally I will ask whether the descriptions of intelligent behavior that were provided in the first part do not justify the making of some distinctions that are either unnoticed or not accorded adequate importance in the arguments outlined in the second part. I shall argue further that these distinctions have important implications for our conclusions concerning both nonhuman intelligent animality and the relationship of humans to other animals and to their own animality. I begin then with descriptions of the activity of one particular kind of highly intelligent animal.

3

The intelligence of dolphins

The intelligent animals with whom I shall be concerned are members of various species of dolphin, especially *Tursiops truncatus*, the bottlenose dolphin, and *Delphinus delphis*, the common dolphin. There are several other types of animal to whom I could have attended—and to some of whom I shall go for occasional examples—chimpanzees, gorillas, dogs, horses, elephants. If I choose dolphins, it is for the following reasons. The activities of dolphins have been the subject of extensive studies (the most important sources for my account of dolphin activity are in *Dolphin Societies: Discoveries and Puzzles*, edd. Karen Pryor and Kenneth S. Norris, Berkeley and Los Angeles: University of California Press, 1991). The ratio of brain mass to body mass is similar to that in anthropoid higher primates, and the cortex is highly developed, although with a different architecture from that of the human cortex. Dolphins live together in groups and herds with well-defined social structures. Although we do not yet understand very much about the sequences of whistles and squeals that they utter, it is clear that they excel at vocal learning and communicate with one another in a variety of ways. They form different types of social bond and exhibit affections and passions. They are subject to fear and to stress. They are purposive, they are playful, and they engage purposefully in play (see K. Martin, K. Shariff, S. Psarakos, and D. J. White 'Ring Bubbles of Dolphins', *Scientific American* 275, 2, August 1996) as well as in hunting and other activities. And although they are a good deal less like human beings than are chimpanzees and gorillas, with whom of course we share much more by way of evolutionary inheritance, they are apt to interact happily with human beings, sometimes initiating the interaction. More important of course is the nature of the interaction of dolphin with dolphin. In a paper primarily concerned to summarize the resources that individual dolphins possess for learning from experience, Louis M. Herman has stressed the need for such learning, if the individual dolphin is to be able to respond to other dolphins in a way that will contribute to her or his flourishing. Their way of life, he says, "places stringent requirements on individuals to learn the identifying characteristics, including behaviors, of many other individuals and how the behaviors of these individuals may be modulated by social and ecological context . . . . In the final analysis, it may be social knowledge that determines the success of the individual dolphin, since the dolphin is dependent on the social matrix for almost all aspects of its life" (Louis M. Herman, op. cit., p. 359; see also K. S. Norris and P. T. Dohl 'The structure and function of cetacean schools' in *Cetacean Behavior: Mechanisms and Functions*, ed. Louis M. Herman, New York: John Wiley and Sons, 1980). That social knowledge is acquired during a progress through a range of relationships from the initial dependence of calves upon mothers to full membership in an adult group.

Dolphins of a variety of species, that is to say, flourish only because they have learned how to achieve their goals through strategies concerted with other members of the different groups to which they belong or which they encounter. The similarities between their strategies in pursuing their goals and the strategies of human beings have been obvious to human observers at least since Aristotle (*History of Animals* 631a7–64).

As with human beings, in order to identify dolphin goals we need to distinguish dolphin actions from mere sequences of bodily movements. With dolphins, as with human beings, the same set of bodily movements may be exhibited in the performance of different actions—jumping purposefully in the course of a hunt and jumping playfully while swimming quietly after a hunt, for example (V. M. Bel'kovich et al., 'Herd Structure, Hunting, and Play', op. cit., pp. 69–70) — and on different occasions the same set of actions may be performed, using different bodily movements—in the course of scouting for the herd during a hunt, for example. And just because actions, unlike sequences of bodily movements, are goal-directed, the successful identification and classification of a great many dolphin actions commits us to an ascription to them of a purposeful pursuit of characteristic goals.

What range of capacities do dolphins exercise in such activities? They include capacities for perceptual recognition, for perceptual attention, for a range of different responses to what is perceived and recognized as the same individual or kind of individual and for a range of varying emotional expressions. Attention may focus first on this and then on that aspect of an object or a set of objects as dolphins exhibit curiosity in inspecting something that has engaged their attention. And the same object or the same kind of object may either be responded to as food or as presenting an opportunity for play. Affection will be expressed towards some individuals who have been recognized, fear towards certain kinds of predator. Cooperation will involve the coordination of one dolphin's actions with those of others in pursuit of a shared goal. So it is insofar as we ascribe such capacities for the exercise of a range of powers that we are also able to ascribe a range of goals to dolphins and further to connect their ability to achieve those goals with their flourishing or failing to flourish in their own specific mode.

Good, said Aquinas, has the *ratio* of a goal (*finis*). A good moves an agent to direct her or his action towards that goal and to treat the achievement of that goal as a good achieved (*Summa Theologiae* Ia 5, 3–5). So humans are goal-directed in virtue of their recognition of goods specific to their nature to be achieved. And, on this Thomistic account at least, since each species has its own goods, the goal-directedness of dolphins seems to provide the same kind of grounds for speaking of the specific and characteristic goods of dolphins as the goal-directedness of human beings provides for speaking of the specific and characteristic goods of human beings. And, just as with human beings, there is a close and observable connection between the successful identification and achievement of particular goods by particular dolphins and those same dolphins flourishing in the specific dolphin mode.

To ascribe goods to dolphins makes it natural also to ascribe to them reasons for doing much that they do. For it is of course in virtue of a similar recognition that we ascribe reasons for much that they do to human beings. Warren Quinn pointed out that "*a reason to act in a certain way is nothing more than something good in itself that it* [the action] *realizes or serves, or, short of that, something bad in itself that it avoids*" ('Putting rationality in its place' in *Morality and Action*, Cambridge: Cambridge University Press, 1993, p. 234, italics in the original). So, if asked to state my reason for acting as I did, I cite the good served by my action, the good towards the realization of which it was directed. What makes my statement true or false is whether my action was or was not in fact directed towards the realization of that particular good, and whether it was or was not in fact so directed is not a matter of what I may have said to myself or to others prior to or at the time of acting, but only a matter of the directedness of my actions by my judgment— often enough unarticulated—about my good.

It is of course the case that sometimes when some human being acts for a reason, she or he does say to her or himself or to others something such as "Doing x will or will not contribute to bringing about y and y is the good that I am aiming to achieve." But what makes it the case that her or his reason for doing x is that x will bring about y is that she or he judges that x will bring about y and that, were she or he to judge otherwise she or he would not do x, unless, that is, there is some other good z that she or he is also aiming to achieve, and she or he also judges that doing x will bring about z. So an agent may possess the relevant beliefs and the actions of that agent may exhibit the relevant goal-directedness without the agent giving utterance to any statement of her or his reasons for so acting.

It is therefore in itself no obstacle to ascribing reasons for their actions to the members of nonhuman intelligent species, such as dolphins, that they do not possess the linguistic resources for articulating and uttering those reasons. What we do need to be able to identify, if we are to ascribe reasons for action to the members of such species, are a set of goods at the achievement of which the members of that species aim, a set of judgments about which actions are or are likely to be effective in achieving those goods and a set of true counterfactual conditionals that enable us to connect the goal-directedness and the judgments about effectiveness. Characteristically we identify all three of these in conjunction with each other. So it is with humans and so it is also with dolphins.

Eating fish is among the goods of dolphin life. Hunting for fish is, unsurprisingly, a key activity. And the accurate description of episodes in the course of hunting commits us to asserting the truth of sets of counterfactual conditionals of exactly the same type as those to which we are committed by accurate descriptions of human activity. Consider, for example, the type of case in which scouts searching for fish on behalf of a herd have detected fish and members of the rest of the herd, recognizing this, change course in swimming, so as to join the scouts and commence the hunt (op. cit., V. M. Bel'kovich et al., 'Herd Structure, Hunting and Play', p. 43). In assigning the reason that the rest of the herd have for changing course, we are asserting both that, had the rest of the herd not recognized that the scouts had detected fish, they would—absent any other reason for changing course—not have changed course, so as to swim to where the scouts were, *and* that, given that the members of the herd were engaged in the preliminaries of a hunt, *either* they would have had to have some other reason of comparable importance for not changing course—for example, they simultaneously discovered fish immediately ahead of them on the course on which they had previously been swimming— *or* they would have had to be physically prevented from changing course, for them not to have changed course in the direction of the scouts.

Or consider how dolphins, while engaged in hunting, will

first adopt one means for achieving their end, but, if they then discover that that means is ineffective, will exchange it for another. So Bel'kovich and his colleagues report episodes such as that in which bottlenose dolphins who have first tried to drive a school of fish towards the shore, in order to pen them in, but who are failing to do so, will then instead drive the fish out to sea towards the rest of the herd. It is of course crucial to this interpretation that we should have adequate grounds for ascribing to dolphins possession of the perceptual and communicative capacities necessary for them to become aware of the relevant facts.

That dolphins do possess such capacities is evidenced not only by their performances in the ocean, but also by what they have shown themselves able to learn from human trainers. Herman's research into those capacities led him to conclude— and I know of no researcher who dissents—"that in its natural world, the dolphin is well prepared to perceive, recognize, categorize, and remember the multitude of sounds and sights it receives through its auditory or visual senses." The importance of sound and of the ability to echolocate for dolphins can scarcely be exaggerated and Herman not only takes it that they learn from experience over time what the sources of different sounds are, with confirmation from visual identification and "through social observation of the responses of others to the sounds," but adds that "in youngsters" learning may be assisted "possibly through some degree of more direct social tutoring by adults" (op. cit., p. 357).

The activities involved in perceptual learning and in then putting to use what they have learned render dolphins no mere passive receptors of experience. And, like human beings, dolphins take pleasure in those activities which are the exercise of their powers and skills. When Aristotle says that there is pleasure in all perceptual activity (*Nicomachean Ethics* X 1174b 20–21) and that the pleasure supervenes upon the completed activity (23–33), what he asserts seems to be as true of dolphins as of human beings (on the sense of achievement and the pleasure taken in achievement by dolphins, see Pryor op. cit., p. 346).

Consider now the full range of powers that have been ascribed to dolphins by some of those with most opportunity to interact with them: not only powers of perception, perceptual attention, recognition, identification and reidentification, but also of having and exhibiting desire and emotion, of making judgments, of intending this and that, of directing their actions towards ends that constitute their specific goods and so having reasons for acting as they do. But if we are justified in making all these ascriptions, we are presumably also justified in ascribing thoughts and beliefs to dolphins. It would be difficult then to avoid the further conclusion that dolphins possess certain concepts and know how to apply them. And at this point therefore the whole range of philosophical arguments whose conclusion is a denial that animals without language can have thoughts, beliefs, reasons for actions or concepts confront us. Yet before we can consider what the bearing of each of the particular arguments is on the interpretation of dolphins and other animal behavior we need first to ask what their authors have meant or mean by 'language'.

No one doubts that dolphins have a sophisticated system of communication. And so of course do chimpanzees, gorillas, and others. In the case of dolphins there is a great deal that we do not as yet understand about their system of communication and so it is still possible that they may turn out to have something very much closer to human language than our present evidence seems to suggest. But they certainly have a remarkable capacity for some type of linguistic comprehension. Louis M. Herman and his colleagues have invented a simple, artificial, acoustical language and have taught dolphins to understand and to respond to sentences in that language. Dolphins thus instructed are able not only to identify a range of objects and of proposed actions referred to in sentences spoken to them, an ability that requires, so Herman reports, responsiveness to syntactical distinctions between sentences and to changes in word-order, but also to discriminate between syntactically deviant and syntactically standard sentences ('What the dolphin knows or might know in its natural world' in Pryor and Norris op. cit., p. 351). But although this is unquestionably an achievement of great significance for evaluating the communicative and linguistic capacities of dolphins, just what that significance is could only emerge from a detailed comparison with what is acquired by human children and with their mode of language acquisition. I therefore for the moment put discussion of this achievement on one side, in order to let the argument proceed in three stages. First I shall offer a rough and ready and incomplete, but, I hope, adequate characterization of some salient and relevant features of human languages. Next I will examine those philosophical arguments that move from premises about the nature of human language to conclusions about the inability of nonhuman animals, no matter how intelligent, to have thoughts, beliefs, reasons for action and concepts. And finally I will ask what the bearing of those arguments, insofar as they are sound, is on the question of how we ought to characterize the intelligent activity of dolphins.

4

Can animals without language have beliefs?

What then are the salient and relevant characteristics of human language, exemplified in the more than four and a half thousand natural languages of human cultures? First, every natural language has a vocabulary, a stock of words, and a stock of expressions, many of them consisting of a string of words ('good at', 'is red') rather than a single word. The speakers of each particular language have a stock of shared phonemes that enable them to pronounce those expressions recognizably and sometimes have a stock of written signs that serve the purpose of written utterance. Secondly, a language has a set of rules for combining expressions, so as to form sentences. These rules constitute the syntax of the language. Simple sentences, decomposable into expressions, but not into further sentences, can be combined in various ways to form further sentences of indefinite length and complexity. Thirdly the types of expression that make up sentences include names, definite descriptions, predicates, quantifiers, demonstratives, pronouns, and such other indexicals as 'here' and 'now', and those logical connectives that make possible negation, disjunction, conjunction, and relations of logical implication, entailment and equivalence. The relationship between a name and its bearer, between a description and that to which it applies, between a demonstrative or a pronoun and that which is referred to by its use and between such indexicals as 'here' and 'now' and the times and places to which they refer have to be understood, if those types of expression are to be understood and to provide a language with its semantic dimension.

Yet having a stock of expressions at one's disposal, knowing how to organize these in accordance with syntactic rules and even being able to match names to bearers ('Fido' to Fido), predicates to properties ('green' to green) and indexicals to this or that to which they refer and so on are not together sufficient for the possession of a language or competence in its use. It is necessary also to be able to use sentences to perform such speech acts (I use 'speech act' to include performances in writing) as those of assertion, of questioning, of requesting or enjoining, of agreeing or promising and the like, and to understand the contexts that make those uses appropriate. And this fourth requirement is not all. One must also know how to perform certain types of linguistic task by the use of speech acts: to announce the solution of a puzzle by making an assertion, to express a doubt by asking a question, to indicate an object of desire by making a request and so on. Uttering syntactically impeccable sentences at regular intervals is not exhibiting an ability to use language. Even using such sentences to utter a series of speech acts is not exhibiting such ability. The use of the sentences in speech acts must serve some further intelligible purpose, intelligible that is in terms both of the agent's situation and purposes and of the social context. It is by uttering a syntactically ordered sentence in such a way that my utterance is some particular type of speech act, performed in such a way that it serves some intelligible purpose (not necessarily, although usually evident to observers with a knowledge of the same language) that I make my meaning known.

Two features of this account of language need especially to be remarked. The first is that on this account the use of a language is always embedded in forms of social practice and to understand adequately what is said on particular occasions in a given language one must have some at least of the abilities of a participant in the relevant form of social practice. In the elementary learning of foreign languages, especially the languages of cultures very close to one's own, this often passes unnoticed. Many of the relevant types of social situation are highly stylized and the sentences used in them presuppose or refer to social situations in ways that already make use of the needed ability (as in phrase-book versions of languages: 'Where is the nearest bus station?' 'What is the price of this book?'). But where there are large differences between cultures a knowledge of how to construct sentences in some alien language unaccompanied by a sufficient degree of knowledge of and ability to participate with understanding in the relevant set of social practices may result in failure in communication and misunderstanding of intentions. Bernard S. Cohn has described (*Colonialism and Its Forms of Knowledge*, Princeton: Princeton University Press, 1996, pp. 18–19) how seventeenth- and eighteenth-century Europeans in India, especially the British, construed gift-giving and gift-receiving in terms of forms of exchange in which "everything and everyone had a 'price'," thus misconstruing the beliefs and intentions that would have been communicated, had the British only been educated into the relevant Indian social practices. Their failure in understanding was not the result of ineptitude in the skills of sentence construction or sentence decomposition. But, it may be asked, why are such examples important for the present argument?

The answer is that with nonhuman animals of those species with which we shall be especially concerned successful communication of beliefs and intentions is as embedded in forms of social practice as it is with human beings. And this is as true of the communication achieved by members of a species with one another in the context of the social life of, say, a herd of dolphins or a pride of lions, as it is of the communication achieved between humans and nonhumans in the very special social contexts provided by training. We need to be careful of course not to compare what members of this or that species of nonhuman animal are capable of in their natural habitat, apart from any contact with humans, with what they turn out to be capable of as a result of training. But, if we observe this caution, we will be able to make important inferences from the latter to the former. Observation of the latter may, for example, enrich our knowledge of the powers possessed by this or that species, so that when we observe activity in a natural habitat we are able to recognize it as an exercise of those powers.

I am well aware of the limited character of what I have said about the various aspects of language and its use under the headings of vocabulary, syntax, semantics, the performance of speech-acts, and embedding in social practice, but it is perhaps sufficient to explain and evaluate the range of claims that philosophers have recently made about what else it is that animals who lack language must also lack. I now turn therefore to those claims and begin with some theses advanced by Norman Malcolm. Malcolm's central preoccupation in the essay in which he advanced these theses ('Thoughtless Brutes', Essay 2, in *Thought and Knowledge*, Ithaca: Cornell University Press, 1977) was with a contention by Justus Hartnack (in 'On Thinking', *Mind* 81, 1972, p. 551) that "there can be no thoughts and no thinking, if there is no language." To this Malcolm responded by distinguishing what it is to ascribe thinking and what it is to ascribe the having of a thought. We can say of a dog who has pursued a cat that has climbed a tree, and who now waits expectantly beneath the tree, that it thinks that the cat is in the tree. But we cannot say of a dog, or of any other being without language, that it has the thought that . . . . For "although we apply the word 'think' to animals, using it as a transitive verb taking a propositional phrase as its object, we do not thereby imply that the animal *formulated* or *thought of* a proposition" (p. 50). Malcolm thus equates having a thought with holding before one's mind some proposition and a proposition must be expressible in language. "I agree therefore with the Cartesians that thoughts cannot be ascribed to animals that are without language" (p. 50).

Yet in an important way Malcolm was not agreeing with the Cartesians. Descartes's denial that animals have thoughts is part of his denial of any mental life to animals. Malcolm gives us no grounds for such a denial. All that he denied was that animals without language could frame propositions and consider them independently of acting on them. And with this no one who used 'proposition' as Malcolm does could disagree. But from nothing Malcolm says does it follow that animals without language may not have, for example, beliefs. Malcolm's dog, it might perhaps be said, believes that the cat is up the tree. It does not need language to express this belief. And of course we humans do not need language to express many of our beliefs either. Moreover the dog then acts on its belief. So it may seem as if we may at least raise the question of whether the belief is not only a cause of the dog's behavior, but provides the dog with a reason for acting as it does. Yet here some larger difficulties arise. For we cannot even frame this question, unless we are entitled to ascribe beliefs to the dog. And a number of different arguments whose conclusion is that we are not entitled to ascribe beliefs to any non-language-using animal have been advanced. Four of them are of particular importance.

Two have been advanced by Donald Davidson in a paper whose chief thesis is "that a creature cannot have thoughts unless it is an interpreter of the speech of another" ('Thought and Talk', chapter 11 of *Truth and Interpretation*, Oxford: Clarendon Press, 1984, p. 157). Davidson's first contention is grounded in an argument whose outcome "suggests that the attribution of desires and beliefs (and other thoughts) must go hand in hand with the interpretation of speech" (p. 163). I know how to determine what another has chosen only if I can also assign the relevant set of beliefs to that other. "A man who takes an apple rather than a pear when offered both may be expressing a preference for what is on his left rather than on his right, what is red rather than yellow, what is seen first, or judged more expensive" (p. 163). And, "if we think of all choices as revealing a preference that one sentence rather than another be true," we will have to recognize that the interpretation of what the other means by her or his sentences and the correct assignment of desires and beliefs are inseparable tasks. But with beings who do not have a capacity for uttering sentences, it will then be impossible to have sufficient grounds for ascribing particular determinate desires or beliefs.

This conclusion leads very naturally to the further question: if we cannot have sufficient grounds for ascribing particular determinate desires or beliefs to non-language-users, can we have grounds for ascribing *any* beliefs to them? A second argument advanced by Davidson may seem to give us conclusive reasons for asserting that we cannot. This argument proceeds in two stages. In the first Davidson concludes that we can only have a concept of belief, if, as members of some speech community, we are engaged in interpreting the speech of others by ascribing beliefs to them. So only those with language can have the concept of belief. Davidson then asks "Can a creature have a belief if it does not have the concept of belief?" (p. 70). His reply is that it cannot, since someone can only have a belief if he or she "understands the possibility of being mistaken," something that requires a grasp of the difference between true and false belief. Hence only those with language can have beliefs.

A third argument that raises difficulties for the ascription of beliefs to animals without language has been formulated by Stephen Stich ('Animal Beliefs' 5.5, *From Folk Psychology to Cognitive Science: The Case Against Belief*, Cambridge, Mass.: MIT Press, 1983; see also his earlier 'Do Animals Have Beliefs?', *Australasian Journal of Philosophy* 57, 1, 1979). Stich's example is the same as Malcolm's, except that the dog, Fido, has now chased a squirrel up an oak tree: "it would be perfectly natural to say he believes that the squirrel is up in the oak tree" (p. 104). But is this really what the dog believes? "Are there not indefinitely many logically possible creatures which are not squirrels but which Fido would treat indistinguishably from the way he treats real squirrels?" Moreover the dog does not distinguish the living from the non-living or animals from plants. "How can you say that he believes that it is a squirrel if he doesn't even know that squirrels are animals?" (p. 105). And the problems that arise over ascribing to the dog a belief about squirrels arises equally over ascribing a belief about trees. Given that the dog does not have a language for which community usage determines the application of 'squirrel' and 'tree', how are we to characterize the dog's belief?

Stich's conclusion, we should note, is interestingly different from Davidson's. Stich compares those writers on animal belief whose focus has been on contrasts "where only rough-and-ready similarity is appropriate" and who have therefore found the ascription of beliefs to animals unproblematic with those—like Davidson—who have attended to "contrasts which stress more fine-grained similarity" (pp. 105–6) and from this have concluded that the ascription of beliefs to animals is mistaken. In his earlier paper Stich's own conclusion had been "that the issue of whether animals have beliefs is moot" (p. 106). But his later conclusion is that in some conversational contexts it may be true to ascribe a belief to a particular animal on a particular occasion, while on others to ascribe the same belief to the same animal in respect of the same evidence would be false.

A fourth argument has been noted by John Searle, although Searle's purpose in presenting it was to argue that it does *not* provide grounds for refusing to attribute intentional states, such as those of belief and desire, to animals without language ('Animal Minds', *Midwest Studies in Philosophy XIX: Philosophical Naturalism*, edd. P. A. French, T. E. Uehling, Jr., and Howard K. Wettstein, Notre Dame: University of Notre Dame Press, 1994, p. 210; I am throughout this discussion much indebted to this paper by Searle). The argument runs as follows. In cases in which we are entitled to ascribe beliefs we can always distinguish between the state of believing that and such other states as those of merely supposing that, guessing that, being inclined on balance to think that, hypothesizing that and so on. But these distinctions have application only to beings who can themselves make such distinctions and only beings with language can do so. Hence the concept of belief itself can have no application to those without language.

What are we to make of these four arguments? Each of them, I shall suggest makes an important point, but none of them provides sufficient grounds for their protagonists' denial of belief to those without language. Let me begin with considering Davidson's argument about truth and falsity. Davidson is of course in the right in contending that only language enables us to reflect upon the truth or falsity of our beliefs, and so to consider reflectively about any particular belief, as to whether it is true or false. But we do not need language to mark the most elementary distinction between truth and falsity. Searle, once again using the example of the dog barking at the cat in the tree, asks: "Why does he now stop barking up the tree and start running towards the neighbor's yard? Because he no longer believes that the cat is up the tree but in the neighbor's yard. Because he just saw (and no doubt smelled) the cat run into the neighbor's yard . . . . The general point is that animals correct their beliefs all the time on the basis of their perceptions" (p. 212). That is, an elementary recognition of the distinction between truth and falsity is embodied in the way in which the animal's belief tracks the changes in the objects of the animal's perception. We, although not the animal, can truly characterize the animal's activity by saying that it recognizes that it is no longer true that . . . . And as it is with animals of many other species, so it is also with us.

For human beings too there is an elementary prelinguistic distinction between truth and falsity embodied in those changes of belief that arise immediately from our perceptions of changes in the world and issue in changes in our activity. When I call this distinction prelinguistic, I do not mean that it only has application in that stage of our early lives when we have not yet learned to speak. Throughout our lives, after we have become able to distinguish the true from the false by a variety of linguistic means, we still continue to distinguish truth from falsity in this prelinguistic way and, were we not able to do so, it is difficult to understand how we would be able to use the words 'true' and 'false' and their cognates as we do. The acquisition of language enables us to characterize and to reflect upon our prelinguistic and nonlinguistic distinction-making in quite new ways, but there is an important continuity between the prelinguistic and linguistic capacities. The former provide matter for characterization by exercise of the latter and in so doing place constraints upon the application of the concepts of truth and falsity that are provided by and in language.

We might be wise then to think of members of certain other species—as various as dogs, dolphins, gorillas, chimpanzees and others—as prelinguistic rather than nonlinguistic. And this is something that we should bear in mind in considering the other three arguments, Davidson's argument to the conclusion that behavior alone must be insufficient to determine which out of a number of possible beliefs (or desires) some being has, Stich's argument for his thesis concerning the semantic indeterminacy of the terms that we use in ascribing beliefs to non-language-using animals, and the argument presented, although not endorsed, by Searle, in which the key premise is that we cannot distinguish in the alleged beliefs of non-language-users different psychological modes of belief, tentative belief from belief without reservation, and the like.

Those three arguments have something in common. What each of them achieves is to show that in some particular respect we cannot ascribe to non-language-using animals beliefs that have the kind of determinacy that the possession and use of language makes possible. The conclusions of these arguments are not of course only about limits on what can be ascribed. They are about limits on what kind of capacities non-language-users can possess. But do these arguments in fact show that non-language-users cannot possess beliefs? I think not and for two different kinds of reason.

Consider first an example. I have been told by an expert that, when a young cat first encounters a shrew, it characteristically and generally treats the shrew exactly as it would a mouse. That is, it tries to catch it, and, if it does so, plays with it, kills it, partly skins it, and eats some. That cat will then become violently ill. Thereafter it will leave shrews severely alone. It now distinguishes between shrews and mice. What its actions show it to believe about shrews is no longer the same as what its actions show it to believe about mice. How should we characterize that cat's change in belief? It is not of course that the cat now believes—and formerly did not—that mice are to be distinguished from shrews in respect of edibility. Davidson's and Stich's arguments remind us that what the cat distinguishes is certainly not precisely the same as what we distinguish in using the terms 'mouse' and 'shrew'. A first approximation might be for us to say of the cat something such as that it now believes that living-objects-of-the-kind-that-we-treat-as-shrews are not-to-be-eaten or are to-be-avoided. But what matters is not so much these cumbrous descriptions—and we might well want to make them more cumbrous—as the fact that we are able in a rough and ready way, even if only in a rough and ready way, to map the cat's distinctions and beliefs on to our distinctions and beliefs and moreover that we can observe the cat through its experiences improving its distinctions and amending its beliefs.

The young cat's belief is also of course indeterminate in other ways. Not having language it does not have quantifiers. We therefore cannot characterize its belief by saying of it either that it believes that all shrews are bad eating for cats or that it believes only that at least some shrews are bad eating for cats. And, as the argument noted by Searle reminds us, we also cannot say that it believes that quite certainly some shrews are bad for cats or that it believes only that very probably some shrews are bad for cats. But it does not follow from these considerations that the cat does not have beliefs or that the cat did not change its beliefs. Indeterminate beliefs are beliefs and changes in indeterminate belief are changes in belief.

Part of the importance of this point emerges in a second line of argument, one that concerns humans rather than cats. For human beliefs are often indeterminate in analogous ways. Consider some of our avoidance attitudes and behavior. We may notice in someone else or in ourselves a tendency to avoid certain types of situation, or encounter, or food, or travel. What kind of belief is presupposed in and by this behavior? It will sometimes turn out to be a belief that is as indeterminate in respect of both quantifiers and mode of belief as the cat's. And to recognize it as such may be a first step, as it cannot be in the case of the cat, in the direction of making that belief more precise or of inviting someone else to make their belief more precise. But the phenomenon of indeterminacy of belief is not all that humans share with some non-language-using animals.

I have already suggested that we can in some, but not in other respects map the beliefs of some types of non-language-using animals on to our own (this is very much the point made by Stich) and we can do so because we can up to a point match our perceptual recognitions, identifications, reidentifications and classifications to theirs. And we have also noted that perceptual investigation and attention often play much the same part for them that they do for us. But now we can go beyond this. Consider the young human child, not yet having the power of language, but already actively investigating the environment, attending, recognizing, reidentifying, distinguishing and classifying and, as a result of these investigations, acting on beliefs and from time to time on changes in its beliefs.

Observing such a child, we match the distinctions that it makes as a result of its recognitions, identifications and classifications to our own and we map its beliefs on to our beliefs, just as we do in the case of certain types of nonhuman animal. In the case of children we all do this with some confidence, indeed sometimes with a good deal more confidence than is warranted, because we know that, when the child does learn to speak and so to articulate its beliefs in sentences and to mark distinctions by the use of adjectives, nouns and verbs, its beliefs and distinctions will turn out to be substantially the same as our own adult beliefs, in all those respects in which we identify sameness and difference. The child of course in acquiring language replaces many of its indeterminate beliefs by determinate beliefs. And, as it does so, it becomes able to correct them and to add to them in new ways. But its beliefs, determinate and indeterminate alike, continue to depend for their content on its stock of recognitions, identifications and discriminatory classifications. And these are shared to a remarkable extent by members of different species, both language-using and non-language-using.

What I hope this account brings out is the twofold way in which some human beliefs and the beliefs of members of some nonhuman species are alike. First, I have suggested that some human beliefs are as indeterminate as the beliefs of dogs or apes or dolphins. We give expression to just such beliefs in the multifarious ways in which we move unreflectively and prereflectively through the natural and social world, comporting our bodies, so that our interactions with things and animals fall out in one way rather than another and giving expression in that comportment to a range of beliefs deriving from our perceptions. At this level of existence how the beliefs of other human beings are to be characterized is sometimes as problematic as it is in the case of dogs, apes, and dolphins.

Secondly, even when, as language-users, we become reflective and are able to utter well-formed sentences about what we have learned through our perceptions, we still rely in very large part on just the same kind of recognitions, discriminations, and exercises of perceptual attention that we did before we were able to make use of our linguistic powers. And that is to say, we rely on and give expression to in our beliefs just the same kinds of recognitions, discriminations, and exercise of perceptual attention that certain types of nonhuman animal also rely on and give expression to in the beliefs that guide their actions. Much that is intelligent animal in us is not specifically human. And this may be obscured, if we suppose that there are sound arguments for the conclusion that no being without language can have or be moved to action by beliefs. But this conclusion, I have suggested, is not afforded justification by the strongest arguments so far adduced in its favor.

Because the threadbare examples of dogs in pursuit of cats or squirrels have so dominated the recent literature, I too have used them. But the case that I have been trying to make would have been much more easily made by reference to examples of the extended activities of dolphins or of gorillas or of chimpanzees, in their natural habitats and in their social relationships, or even of dogs participating in more complex relationships and engaged in more demanding activities. And to strengthen and to extend that case it will be necessary to consider just such examples, including examples of capacities exhibited in and as a result of certain types of interaction between humans and nonhumans. Consider one such. Bottlenose dolphins who had learned to understand sentences in the artificial acoustic language invented by Herman and his colleagues could not only distinguish the sentence "Take the surfboard to the frisbee" from the sentence "Take the frisbee to the surfboard," but could also understand some novel instructions conveyed by new combinations of words in familiar syntactical order, and even, in a few cases, instructions that involved hitherto unfamiliar extensions of the syntactical rules (op. cit.).

Part of the interest of these reports is that they show us how the ability of dolphins to recognize references to objects may come to take linguistic form. And it could only do so because of their prelinguistic capacities. That dolphins, like humans, can identify and reidentify objects perceptually prior to any understanding of language is a necessary condition of their later coming to grasp the referential dimensions of the uttered sentences that some of them have learned to understand from Herman and his colleagues. Their perceptual habits and activities had prepared them for, had brought them to the verge of, linguistic understanding.

What I am suggesting then is that adult human activity and belief are best understood as developing out of, and as still in part dependent upon, modes of belief and activity that we share with some other species of intelligent animal, including dolphins, and that the activities and beliefs of members of those species need to be understood as in important respects approaching the condition of language-users. And I have claimed that the arguments advanced against the very possibility of animals without language having beliefs do not warrant this conclusion. But these are not the only arguments that have to be confronted.

5

How impoverished is the world of the nonhuman animal?

The philosophers whom I have discussed so far all belong to one or other version of the analytic tradition in philosophy. But this is not the only tradition within which sharp and, I believe, obscurantist lines have been drawn between nonhuman animals and human beings. Just such a line was drawn by Heidegger in his lecture course in 1929-30 (published in English translation by W. McNeill and N. Walker as *The Fundamental Concepts of Metaphysics: World, Finitude, Solitude*, Bloomington and Indianapolis: Indiana University Press, 1995). Earlier in *Sein und Zeit* Heidegger had only made passing reference to nonhuman animals. (Heidegger uses *'Tier'*, in line with ordinary German usage, to refer exclusively to nonhuman animals. So in discussing his views I shall, like his translators, use 'animal' wherever he uses or would have used *'Tier'*.) And later in the *Letter on Humanism* in 1946 he would refer to the "scarcely fathomable, abyssal" character of the "bodily kinship" of humans to animals. But it is only in the 1929-30 lectures that there is any extended discussion.

Heidegger's conclusions are radical. The human being is 'world-forming' (*weltbildend*), the stone is altogether 'without world' (*weltlos*), and the animal is 'poor in world' (*weltarm*) (§49–50). This poverty is expressed in the fact that an animal "can only behave [*sich . . . benehmen*] but can never apprehend [*vernehmen*] something as something—which is not to deny that the animal sees or even in some sense perceives. Yet in a fundamental sense the animal does not have perception" (p. 259). What is it that the animal lacks?

The animal is captive to its environment. In that environment it encounters "that which disinhibits . . . the instinctual drive" and "thus allows the animal to move within certain instinctual drives" (pp. 255–56). But that which thus triggers behavior by bringing the instinctual drive into play "is *nothing enduring* that could *stand over against the animal as a possible object*" (p. 256). The animal has an "essential inability to attend to" (p. 256) that which released its instinctual drive. Its being thus taken hold of by some aspect of its environment "never involves an attending to beings" (p. 259). What is this incapacity for attention?

Heidegger's discussion, unlike those of his English-speaking analytic counterparts, uses examples drawn from a wide range of types of animal. A domesticated dog does appear early in the discussion, but thereafter we find a welcome variety of bees, moths, freshwater crabs, lizards, sea-urchins, woodworms, and woodpeckers and, when a squirrel does appear, it is not chased by a dog, but startled by a woodpecker. What we do not find are wolves or elephants or, even more importantly, gorillas or chimpanzees or dolphins. Why this selection of animal examples is important will only emerge when we consider the grounds for Heidegger's conclusions about animal incapacity for attention. But we do need to note immediately that, although Heidegger's examples concern only certain species of animal, his conclusions are about nonhuman animals as such. Why then is it that such animals do not possess the power of "attending to beings"?

What animals lack is any apprehension of that to which they relate "*as* something," "*as* something present to hand, *as* a being" (p. 248). The lizard lying on the rock may have some awareness of the rock, but not *as a rock* (p. 198). The bee is guided in its flight by light, but is not aware of the light that impinges on it *as light* (p. 247). Beings make themselves manifest to human beings *as* what they are in each particular case. They do not thus manifest themselves to animals. Hence animals cannot attend to beings, for beings are not presented to them. And since to form a world and to have a world requires such presentation, animals are poor in world, not utterly without world, as the rock is, but possessing only a deprived and impoverished form of experience.

Being poor in world is inseparable from, indeed derives from (p. 271) being captive to one's environment, a captivity that involves "absorption in the totality of interacting instinctual drives," being "absorbed into its drivenness" (p. 259). So what Heidegger calls the *"qualitative otherness* of the animal world" (p. 264) is bound up with a kind of relationship of the organism to its environment in which the organism cannot free itself from "the encircling ring" of the environment, but is released into activity only as the environment disinhibits its drives. How should we evaluate this characterization of "the animal world"?

It is defective in two distinct, but related ways. It rests first of all on a characterization of nonhuman animals *as such* and its underlying assumption is that the differences between nonhuman species are of no importance or almost no importance in any relevant respect. So it does not matter from which particular species examples are drawn. And I already drew attention to the way in which Heidegger's selection of examples is one-sided. Why should Heidegger have treated the entire realm of nonhuman animals as homogeneous in this way? It is because, so he insists, we can *only* understand nonhuman animals by contrast with our own human condition and what all nonhuman animals share is a lack of what human beings have: a relationship to beings in which not only are beings disclosed, but the difference between beings and being is disclosed. That relationship depends upon the ability of human beings to apprehend what they apprehend *"as such and such."*

The "as" that nonhuman animals lack is the "as" without which there cannot be *logos*, discourse (pp. 312–15). So that for Heidegger, just as for those analytic philosophers who have denied the possibility of belief to nonhuman animals, the presence or absence of language is of crucial importance. But it would be wrong to understand Heidegger as anticipating Davidson in this, and this not only because the account of language that Heidegger was engaged in developing is so very different from Davidson's account. It is rather that for Heidegger the fundamental lack of nonhuman animals is—at least in these lectures—not language itself, but the conceptual capacity that makes language possible, what Heidegger calls "the as-structure."

The thesis that nonhuman animals lack the as-structure is compelling in the case of moths, crabs, lizards, and the like. But it is much more open to question, when we consider dogs, chimpanzees, gorillas, dolphins, and a number of others. First note that members of these species characteristically engage in a range of types of activity ignored by Heidegger: they do not merely respond to features of their environment, they actively explore it; they devote perceptual attention to the objects that they encounter, they inspect them from different angles, they recognize the familiar, they identify and classify, they may on occasion treat one and the same object first as something to be played with and then as something to be eaten, and some of them recognize and even grieve for what is absent. Most important of all, they exhibit in their activity belief-presupposing and belief-guided intentions and they are able to understand and to respond to the intentions communicated by others, both the intentions of other members of their own species and the intentions of humans. For members of some of these species vision is important in just the way that it is for humans. For others, for dolphins, for example, hearing is a more important sense. And for yet others the sense of smell plays a remarkable part. But while these sensory differences may make it difficult on occasion to *imagine* how some animals apprehend what they apprehend, the limitations of imagination should not be allowed to obscure the extent to which and the ways in which the perceptual and intentional achievements of such animals are obscured and misconstrued from Heidegger's perspective.

Heidegger is of course quite right in some of the claims that he makes about nonhuman animals. Such animals cannot grasp the world as a whole. They cannot stand back from their immediate environment. (They notably lack those conceptions of a remembered past and an envisaged future that only the possession of language makes possible, and so they cannot put the present in a temporal context.) Their apprehension of beings is in many respects different from ours. But Heidegger's picture of the nonhuman animal as merely captive to its encircling environment, released into activity only by those features of that environment which disinhibit its instinctual drives, while the human being by contrast is freed up from such captivity by its conceptual and linguistic powers, is a piece of rhetorical exaggeration. Animals of some of the species ignored by Heidegger do not have a single 'encircling' environment. They move between environments and what each such environment is for them is in part constituted by their own modes of apprehension of it and interaction with it.

It is a commonplace about human beings that there are important respects in which we cannot characterize their environments adequately, if we do not take some account of the terms in which at least certain features of those environments are construed by them. But something analogous seems to hold for members of some nonhuman species. Their attention is selective and their environment is partly constituted by what their explorations and their findings make salient for them. We have the same kind of reason as we have in the case of some human beings for concluding that their environment is not simply given as a set of constraints and of arousing stimuli. And this is not the only respect in which Heidegger's account is misleading.

The type of nonhuman animal ignored by Heidegger discriminates particulars, recognizes individuals, notices their absences, greets their returns, and responds to them *as* food or *as* source of food, *as* partner in or material for play, *as* to be accorded obedience or looked to for protection and so on. In so acting such animals—dolphins or gorillas or whatever—

exhibit, even if only in elementary form, just that as-structure which Heidegger takes to be the exclusive possession of human beings. Such nonhuman animals, that is, encounter the particular as a 'this-such'. (It is no accident that at this point the terminology becomes Aristotelian. Heidegger's elucidation of the as-structure is itself presented as exegesis of Aristotle.) They classify it and they respond to it on this occasion *as* being of this kind and on another *as* also having this or that property and sometimes on the same occasion *as* being of more than one kind. With respect to how precisely we characterize such animals' classifications and identifications we need to bear in mind the caution enjoined by Stich. But, even if we are appropriately cautious, we will still find numerous cases in which we need to use 'as' in contexts in which Heidegger was committed to denying that it has application.

Heidegger's mistake was, by ascribing a single condition to all nonhuman animals, to lose sight of crucial differences between them. The differences between earthworms, crabs, and woodpeckers on the one hand (and the differences between each of these species are themselves not insignificant) and apes, dogs, and dolphins on the other (again the differences between *them* should not escape notice) are not only important in their own right, but, if we fail to give them their due, we will also fail to understand adequately what the significance of the difference between human beings and some other intelligent species is. And this is Heidegger's second failure. It is not just that he misdescribed nonhuman animals. It is also that in consequence he omitted to notice crucial aspects of *Dasein*, human existence. And his omissions are not unrelated to those of some of the analytic philosophers whom I have discussed.

What I already stressed then in respect of the relationship between human beliefs and the beliefs of some nonhuman animals was the extent to which the development of some distinctively human language-using powers and capacities extends and is founded upon animal powers and capacities shared with members of some other intelligent species. I now want to amplify this claim. It is not only that the same kind of exercise of the same kind of perceptual powers provides, guides, and corrects beliefs in the case of dolphins—and some other species—as in the case of humans, but that our whole initial bodily comportment towards the world is originally an animal comportment and that when, through having become language-users, we under the guidance of parents and others restructure that comportment, elaborate and in new ways correct our beliefs and redirect our activities, we never make ourselves independent of our animal nature and inheritance. Partly this is a matter of those aspects of our bodily condition that simply remain unchanged, of what remains constant through and after the social and cultural scheduling and ordering of our bodily functions: toilet training, developing what one's culture regards as regular sleeping and eating habits, and learning what constitutes politeness and what rudeness by way of sneezing, spitting, burping, farting, and the like. And partly it is a matter of what is involved in our becoming able to reflect upon our overall comportment and our directedness towards the goods of our animal nature, and so in consequence to correct and redirect ourselves, our beliefs, feelings, attitudes, and actions. For it is of the first importance that what we thereby become are redirected and remade animals and not something else. Our second culturally formed language-using nature is a set of partial, but only partial, transformations of our first animal nature. We remain animal selves with animal identities. Heidegger's omissions and exclusions from his account of nonhuman animals are such as to obscure this from view. I take it that it is no accident that on those later occasions when Heidegger wanted to stress the kinship between nonhuman and human animals rather than the extent of the difference between them, what he said was, even for Heidegger, enigmatic and cryptic. He had left himself with no way of saying what needed to be said. But more is at stake here than the criticism of Heidegger.

What I have tried to achieve in the discussion both of theses drawn from analytic philosophy and of Heidegger's claims is not only to engage with the particular arguments, but also more generally to undermine the cultural influence of a picture of human nature according to which we are animals and in addition something else. We have, on this view, a first animal nature and *in addition* a second distinctively human nature. The force of the 'and' is to suggest that this second nature can, at least in the most important respects, only be accounted for in its own terms. Its relation to our given biological nature is thought of as external and contingent in a way and to a degree that permits a single sharp line to be drawn between human beings and members of all nonhuman species. And that line is the line between those who possess language and those who do not. It is of course right to insist upon the significance of the differences between language-possessing and non-language-possessing animals. And some of these will be of crucial importance for my enquiry. But what exclusive, or almost exclusive, attention to these differences may and commonly does obscure is the significance of the continuity and resemblances between some aspects of the intelligent activities of nonhuman animals and the language-informed practical rationality of human beings.

This is not the only way in which the significance of the relevant continuities and resemblances may be obscured. Some of those students of animal behavior who are most anxious to emphasize what dolphins and chimpanzees have in common with human beings perhaps exaggerate how much turns on whether or not such intelligent animals already have or are capable of acquiring—and, if so, to what extent—a fully-fledged language with its own syntax and semantics. These are undeniably questions of the greatest possible interest and they have generated research programs that have been impressively productive in a number of areas. Consider for example what has been discovered about vocal learning by dolphins and the functions of that learning.

Bottlenose dolphins "produce whistles, clicks and burst-pulsed sounds that are all modifiable by experience" (Vincent M. Janik and Peter J. B. Slater 'Vocal Learning in Mammals', *Advances in the Study of Behavior*, vol. 26, New York: Academic Press, 1997, p. 67; Janik and Slater provide a synoptic view of research findings and bibliography for a number of species, including bottlenose dolphins. I am merely and briefly summarizing what they report). From infancy bottlenose dolphins are capable of vocal learning. They have powers of mimicry. They have a large repertoire of whistles, but each individual mostly produces whistles of a form peculiar to itself, its signature whistle. Signature whistles are stable through time and provide a means for individual recognition and reidentification, thus making extended social relationships possible. Imitations of signature whistles "could be used to maintain social bonds or deceive other individuals alike" (Janik and Slater, pp. 66–68, 81, 83, 79).

What has been discovered does not, as yet, provide evidence for any strong thesis about the possession of a fully-fledged language by bottlenose dolphins, even when we add to it the remarkable aptitude for learning the elements of an artificial language disclosed by the work of Herman and his colleagues. But what such dolphins lack by way of language is not what we should be attending to. What is instructive is the use to which they are able to put their vocal learning in exhibiting their prelinguistic expressive powers, their capacities for activity informed by recognition, by belief and by correction of belief, by intentions, activity carried through in concert and communication with others. It is just because these powers are not linguistic, but prelinguistic, that they put in question the single sharp line between those who possess language and those who do not. For the exercise of some of these prelinguistic powers provides what in human beings becomes a crucial subject matter for language. And nowhere is this connection between the prelinguistic and the linguistic more striking than in the relationship between prelinguistic reasons for action and the types of reason for action made possible only by the possession of language.

6

Reasons for action

Anthony Kenny has denied that nonhuman animals can have reasons for their actions. He does so in the course of an exposition of Aquinas's account of voluntariness and an explanation of why Aquinas denied that the acts of nonhuman animals can be voluntary in the way in which human actions are. Both human and nonhuman animals employ means to achieve their ends. They do one thing in order to bring about something else. In the case of a human being that what he or she is doing will bring about that something else is his or her reason for acting as he or she does; but in the case of a nonhuman animal, whose action is also a means to achieving some goal, not so. "Since he lacks a language, he cannot give a reason; and only those beings who can give reasons can act for reasons. Humans are rational, reason-giving animals; cats and dogs are not, and therefore cannot act for reasons" (*Aquinas on Mind*, London: Routledge, 1993, p. 82).

Why does the absence of language have this effect? (Kenny is careful to note that in giving this kind of importance to language, he is expressing his own view and not Aquinas's. For an excellent overview of Aquinas's discussion of animals see Judith A. Barad, *Aquinas on the Nature and Treatment of Animals*, San Francisco: International Scholars Publications, 1995.) It is because without language an animal cannot evaluate that which moves it to action. It cannot ask whether its reason for acting as it does is a good reason and so it does not, on Kenny's view, have a reason. Aquinas had denied to nonhuman animals the freedom that he ascribes to human animals, on the grounds that "Judgment is in the power of someone judging to the extent that one can pass judgment on one's own judging; for whatever is in our power is something about which we can make a judgment. But to pass judgment on one's own judgment belongs only to reason . . ." (*De Veritate* 24, 2). And about the significance of the power to pass judgment on our judgments as a mark of both rationality and voluntariness Aquinas is plainly right.

Human practical rationality certainly has among its distinctive features the ability to stand back from one's initial judgments about how one should act and to evaluate them by a variety of standards. Moreover Kenny is also right in claiming that this ability can only be exercised by language-users. But what is required for the exercise of this ability is not just language, but a type of language that has the resources necessary for the formation of sentences with a certain degree of complexity.

Those who have wanted to draw a single sharp line between human and nonhuman animals have commonly laid emphasis upon the presence or absence of language as such, the ability to use and to respond to strings of syntactically ordered and semantically significant expressions whose utterance constitutes speech acts. But this is insufficient for human rationality. What is needed in addition is the ability to construct sentences that contain as constituents either the sentences used to express the judgment about which the agent is reflecting or references to those sentences. Where my reason for acting is or has been of the form 'Doing x will enable me to achieve y' where 'y' stands for some good, reflection on this reason will require me to ask 'In this type of situation do I have a better reason for acting than that doing x will enable me to achieve y?' I will have to compare *this* as a reason for acting with alternative reasons for alternative actions. So there might perhaps be some animal species whose members or some of whose members were capable of acquiring language, but at a level of complexity less than that required for this kind of practical rationality. If there is, and if Kenny's argument is sound, then we would not be justified in saying even of such language users that they were capable of having reasons for acting as they do. But is Kenny's argument sound? Is his conclusion perhaps too strong?

Aquinas's conclusions are interestingly different from Kenny's. Aristotle had remarked on the difference between the *phronesis* of humans and that of other animals, while observing that we do ascribe *phronesis* to members of certain other species (*Nicomachean Ethics* VI, 1141a 22–28). And Jean-Louis Labarrière has argued that what Aristotle had in mind is a relationship in some nonhuman animals between their perceptions and the imperatives that govern their actions that implies "un analogue de raisonnement (une sorte de pensée pratique)" ('De la Phronesis Animale' in *Biologie, Logique et Metaphysique chez Aristote*, Séminaire CNRS-N. S. F., 1987, Paris: Editions du CNRS, 1990, p. 417).

Aquinas follows Aristotle in this. Nonhuman animals are, he allowed, "moved by precepts" and on occasion learn from past experience to recognize this or that as friendly or hostile. In virtue of their nature and of such capacity for learning as they have, they are able to make what Aquinas calls "natural judgments." So they do exhibit what Aquinas calls "a semblance of reason" and "they share in" what he calls "natural prudence." Hence, when Aquinas speaks of the judgment of nonhuman animals and asserts that they act from judgment (*De Veritate*, response to the seventh objection, 24, 2; see also *Summa Theologiae* Ia, 84, 1), he is using this term by analogy with human reflective judgment, even although nonhuman animals do not have the same power of judgment as human beings. The wolf and the sheep have reasons for acting as they do, even although they do not have the power of reason. (This analogical predication, we should note, can only be employed justifiably, if we are able to ascribe certain conceptual capacities—an ability to recognize sameness and difference of kind, for example—to the relevant types of nonhuman animal, in just the same sense as that in which we ascribe them to human beings.)

Aquinas's conclusion is thus weaker than Kenny's. We do

indeed need to mark the difference between the kind of reason for action that some nonhuman animals have and the kind of reasons that language-using, reflective human beings have. But we need not and should not deny that on occasion such nonhuman animals in some sense have reasons for acting as they do. The premises from which Kenny argues warrant this weaker conclusion, but not his own stronger version. Why is this important?

It is because any exercise of the power to reflect on our reasons for action presupposes that we already have such reasons about which we can reflect, prior to our reflection. And for us human beings it is because we do have reasons for action prior to *any* reflection, the kinds of reason that we share with dolphins and chimpanzees, that we have an initial matter for reflection, a starting point for that transition to rationality which a mastery of some of the complexities of language use can provide. Did we not share such reasons with dolphins and chimpanzees we would not have arrived at that starting point and a denial that we have such reasons would render the transition to specifically human rationality unintelligible. In early childhood, that is to say, human beings have not yet made the transition from being only potentially rational animals to being actually rational animals. (Here I put on one side questions about the nature of that evolutionary transformation by which some intelligent primates first moved from being intelligent animals to being rational animals.) The first step in this transition takes place when a child becomes able to consider the suggestion that the good to the achievement of which it is presently directed by its animal nature is inferior to some other alternative good and that this latter good therefore provides a better reason for action than does the good at which the child has been aiming. And this is possible only if there is indeed some good at which it has been aiming, a good that has provided it with a reason for action. Human infants, like dolphins, have prelinguistic reasons for actions, and the complexity of the relationships between the goods that they pursue and the means that they adopt in order to achieve them matches that exhibited by dolphin reasoning. But they go beyond the reasoning characteristic of dolphins when they become able to reflect on and to pass judgment on the reasons by which they have hitherto been guided. This transition is one that dolphins have not made, so far as we know, but we can learn a good deal from them—and from chimpanzees and members of various other species—about the preconditions for making it.

To acknowledge that there are these animal preconditions for human rationality requires us to think of the relationship of human beings to members of other intelligent species in terms of a scale or a spectrum rather than of a single line of division between 'them' and 'us'. At one end of this scale there are types of animal for whom sense perception is no more than the reception of information without conceptual content. There is, in Heidegger's terms, no 'as-structure' whatsoever. At another level are animals whose perceptions are in part the result of purposeful and attentive investigation and whose changing actions track in some way the true and the false. And among such animals we can distinguish between those whose perceptions and responses are more fine-grained and those whose perceptions and responses are less so.

Differences in the type of intention exhibited in behavior and communicated to others are also important in placing different species on this scale. And a further point is reached, when we are able to conclude, as, for example, Hauser and Nelson do with respect to chimpanzees that "nonhuman animals are capable both of withholding information and of falsely signaling about objects and events in the environment" (Marc D. Hauser and Douglas A. Nelson, "'Intentional' Signaling in Animal Communication," *Trends in Ecology and Evolution* 6, 6, June 1991, p. 189. On how we should characterize nonhuman animal deception also see Marc D. Hauser, 'Minding the behavior of deception' in *Machiavellian Intelligence II,* edd. A. W. Whiten and R. W. Byrne, Cambridge: Cambridge University Press, 1997; other essays in this volume and in its 1988 predecessor *Machiavellian Intelligence: Social Expertise and the Evolution of Intellect in Monkeys, Apes, and Humans—*

same editors, same publisher—provide excellent examples of nonhuman primate activities that warrant, from the standpoint that I have taken, ascriptions not only of intelligence, but of intentions, of predictive capacity and of reasons provided by that predictive capacity for forming one intention rather than another. An excellent overview is provided by Robin Dunbar in 'The Ghost in the Machine', chapter 5 of his *Grooming, Gossip, and the Evolution of Language*, London: Faber & Faber and Cambridge, Mass.: Harvard University Press, 1996). With such chimpanzees, as with dolphins, we have reached a point on the scale at which we find those species some of whose members are capable of different degrees of sophisticated interaction with human beings, interactions in which the perceptions, beliefs, reasons for action, and intentions of the nonhuman participants play very much the same part as do the perceptions, beliefs, reasons for action, and intentions of the human participants.

Human beings do of course stand at a still further point on the scale, one marked not merely by language, but by an ability to put language to certain kinds of reflective use. But this does not remove from us what we share with other animal species. Our kinship to the dolphin and the chimpanzee cannot be discarded and this is a kinship not only with respect to the animality of the body, but also with respect to forms of life. The greatest students of animal behavior have exercised skills and sensibilities that resemble closely those of the gifted social or cultural anthropologist. They have been able to teach us—at least up to a point—what it is like to be a dog, a horse, a gorilla, a dolphin. (Thomas Nagel is right to insist that we do not know what it is like to be a bat, but this is not only because of their perceptual reliance on echolocation, but also because the difference between their form of life and ours is so much more radical than the differences between us and other primates or dolphins. See 'What is it like to be a bat?' in *Mortal Questions*, Cambridge: Cambridge University Press, 1979.) Wittgenstein remarked that "If a lion could speak, we could not understand him" (*Philosophical Investigations* II, xi, 223). About lions perhaps the question has to be left open. But I am strongly inclined to say of dolphins that, even although their modes of communication are so very different from ours, it is nonetheless true that if they could speak, some of the greatest of the recent interpreters of dolphin activity would be or would have been able to understand them.

The conception of ourselves, dolphins, chimpanzees, dogs, bats, lizards, and spiders as at different points on a scale is also important in another way (note that the placing of these species at different points on one and the same scale is not at all incompatible with a recognition of their very different evolutionary histories). At the lower points on that scale perception plays a part in the causation of behavior, perhaps as information-affording, but not because it is reason-affording. At higher points what part perception plays in causing behavior sometimes varies with just how far it is reason-affording or is taken to be reason-affording. Dolphins, for example, on occasion misconstrue what they perceive. They respond as to a predator, when what is present is not a predator. But it is as they take their perceptions to be reason-affording that they respond by acting in one way rather than another. And when a species, such as our own, is able through the use of language to become reflective about its reasons, it is not only the having of reasons that is now on occasion causally effective in guiding behavior, but the having of reasons for taking this set of considerations rather than that to be in this particular situation genuinely reason-affording that is causally effective.

The causal relations between animals and their environment are thus of a number of different kinds and the explanation of animal behavior is different at different points in the scale, as more and more weight has to be given in those explanations to the ways in which different species take account of features of their environment in developing complex forms of purposeful behavior. And this is obscured, if we insist on ignoring or minimizing the analogies between the intelligence exhibited in dolphin activities or chimpanzee activities and the rationality exhibited in human activities, as, for example, Hans-Georg

Gadamer does, when—following Heidegger—he insists that
nonhuman animals, lacking language ("Animals have language
only *per aequivocationem*," *Truth and Method*, New York: The
Seabury Press, 1975, p. 403) can never sever "their environ-
mental dependence," while humans by contrast are able to
adopt "a free, distanced attitude" towards the environment, or
as John McDowell does, when, after endorsing Gadamer, he
asserts that "In mere animals, sentience is in the service of a
mode of life that is structured exclusively by immediate biological imperatives" and that "merely animal life is shaped by goals
whose control of the animal's behavior at a given moment is an
immediate outcome of biological forces" (*Mind and World*,
Cambridge, Mass.: Harvard University Press, 1994, Lecture
VI, p. 115; for criticism of McDowell's view see John Haldane,
'Rational and Other Animals' in *Verstehen and Human Understanding* Cambridge: Cambridge University Press, 1996, and
Gerald Vision, 'Perceptual Content', *Philosophy* 73, July, 1998,
especially section VII).

McDowell says later that "Human beings are born mere
animals, and they are transformed into thinkers and intentional
agents in the course of coming to maturity" (p. 125) and, as a
result of acquiring language, learning "what is a reason for
what" (p. 126). It has been my claim that on the type of view
taken by Gadamer and McDowell this transformation may be in
danger of becoming unintelligible, that it is only because some
of what McDowell calls "mere animals" are already guided by a
kind of practical reasoning that is exhibited in their taking *this*
to be a reason for doing *that*, one that is to be characterized by
analogy with human understanding, that some of the prelinguistic conditions necessary for the development of human
rationality—conditions satisfied by members of some nonhuman species as well as by human beings—are satisfied. Dolphins, gorillas, and members of some other species are no more
merely responsive to the inputs of their senses than we are. They
too inhabit a world whose salient features can have this or that
significance for them. They too respond on the basis of their

classifications and interpretations. They too make and correct mistakes.

Different as they are in important respects from language-using human beings, they are able to form relationships not only with members of their own species, but also with human beings, and to decipher the interactions and purposes of those human beings, while giving expression to their own intentions and purposes. So that the relationships of some nonhuman animals to some human animals are far more clearly analogous to human relationships than some of the philosophical theorizing that I have discussed would allow. Some human beings indeed and some nonhuman animals pursue their respective goods in company with and in cooperation with each other. And what we mean by 'goods' in saying this is precisely the same, whether we are speaking of human or dolphin or gorilla.

7

Vulnerability, flourishing, goods, and 'good'

Dolphins, during what would otherwise be their relatively long lives, are vulnerable to a variety of lethal agents: diseases, injuries, predators, malnutrition, and starvation caused by damage to their feeding-grounds, and most recently the devastating activities of fishing crews, sometimes incidentally, as with the purse seining of crews in pursuit of high profits from yellowfin tuna, and sometimes through the hunting of dolphin for the dolphin meat market. Against many of these threats they can do nothing to protect themselves. But there seems little doubt that the chances of dolphins surviving and flourishing are remarkably enhanced by the ways in which at different stages of their lives, their social relationships are structured by membership in groups—groups of females with their calves, groups of subadult males, groups of older male and female dolphins—and by the formation of alliances.

When we identify the harms and dangers to which dolphins are exposed and the nature of their vulnerability to those harms and dangers, we presuppose a certain notion of dolphin flourishing, of what it would be for an individual dolphin to flourish as a member of various groups in turn during a life in which the activities and achievements of natural and normal development were exemplified. The particular goods achieved by different types of activity—the activity of hunting, that of feeding, that of play, that of sexual activity—are identified as goods both because they are objects of directed activity and so of desire, the satisfaction of which completes the activity, and also because they contribute to and are partially constitutive of such well-being. And it is insofar as something tends to interfere with or to be an obstacle to the achievement of such particular goods or of flourishing in general that it is accounted a harm or a danger.

I have already argued that, when by acting in such and such a way a dolphin will achieve some such particular good, it may be said to have a reason for so acting, and that, when it is because that dolphin perceives that by so acting it will achieve that particular good, it may be said to act for a reason. When we thus ascribe reasons for action to dolphins or to members of other non-language-using species, we do so, I earlier suggested, by analogy with our ascriptions of reasons to human agents. But when we speak of dolphins flourishing or failing to flourish *qua* dolphins or of gorillas flourishing or failing to flourish *qua* gorillas or of humans flourishing or failing to flourish *qua* humans, we use the various parts of the verb 'to flourish' in one and the same sense. These are examples not of analogical, but of univocal predication. What it is to flourish is not of course the same for dolphins as it is for gorillas or for humans but it is one and the same concept of flourishing that finds application to members of different animal—and plant—species. And correspondingly it is one and the same concept of needs that finds similar broad application. What a plant or an animal needs is what it needs to flourish *qua* member of its particular species. And what it needs to flourish is to develop the distinctive powers that it possesses *qua* member of that species.

Whether or not a given individual or group is or is not flourishing *qua* member or members of whatever plant or animal species it is to which it or they belong is in itself a question of fact, even though the question of what it is to flourish has to be answered in part through evaluative and conceptual enquiry. As a question of fact it receives answers in a variety of scientific contexts. Distinguishing between environments in which members of some particular species flourish and environments in which they fail to flourish and distinguishing within some particular population those individuals or groups of a particular species that are flourishing from those that are not is a necessary preliminary to framing certain types of explanatory question which we provided with answers by the biological and ecological sciences. Drawing these distinctions successfully involves identifying the various characteristics that an individual or population of some particular species needs in order to flourish in this or that particular environment, at this or that particular stage of development. But when we say of that individual or group or population that it or they are flourishing is to say more than that it or they possess those characteristics. Yet to flourish is always to flourish *in virtue of* possessing some such set of characteristics. And the concept of flourishing in this respect resembles other concepts that involve applications of the more fundamental concept of good ('to flourish' translates *eu zen* and *bene vivere*).

If we are to understand how this use of 'good' relates to other uses, we need first of all to consider three distinct ways in which we ascribe goodness. We may assert of some type of food that it would be good for you to eat, meaning that it would be good for you to eat it *qua* human being—anyone's health would benefit from eating it or anyone would enjoy eating it. But we may make the same assertion, meaning that it would be good for you to eat *qua* athlete about to undertake a marathon or *qua* recovering invalid. Good is ascribed, that is, both to what benefits human beings as such and to what benefits human beings in particular roles within particular contexts of practice. A good human being is one who benefits her or himself and others (much more will of course need to be said about this) both *qua* human being and also characteristically *qua* the exemplary discharge of particular roles or functions within the context of particular kinds of practice, as someone may benefit her or himself and others both *qua* conscientious and cheerful human being and *qua* shepherd or nurse.

Contrast with 'good human being' and 'good shepherd' 'good thief'. Someone can be a good shepherd without being a good human being, but the goods of sheep farming are genuine

Robin Hood?

goods. To be a good thief however is to be a bad human being. In calling someone a good thief we appraise her or his skills. But even if we judge, as we should, that it may be good to possess these skills, we are not at all committed to asserting that it is good to put them to the use to which the thief puts them. This suggests at least a three-fold classification of ascriptions of good.

There are first of all those ascriptions of good by which we evaluate something *only* as a means. To possess certain skills, to be afforded certain opportunities, to be at certain places at certain times is a good, if and insofar as it enables one to be or do or have some further good. These things are good only *qua* means to something further that is itself good. Consider now a second type of ascription of goodness. To judge someone good in some role or at discharging some function within some socially established practice is to judge that agent good insofar as there are goods internal to that activity that are genuine goods, goods that are to be valued as ends worth pursuing for their own sake, if they are to be pursued at all. Whether there are and what they are is characteristically and generally something to be learned only by being initiated into this or that particular activity. To be excellent in achieving the goods of this or that particular practice is to be good *qua* member of a fishing crew or *qua* mother of a family or *qua* chess player or soccer player. It is to value and to make available goods that are worthwhile for their own sake. Yet for each individual there is the question of whether it is good for her or him that the goods of this or that particular practice should have this or that place in her or his life. And for every society there is the question of whether it is good for that society that the goods of this or that particular practice should have this or that place in its common life. So we need to make a third type of judgment.

It may well be best for me and for others that some set of goods—genuine goods—should have a subordinate place or no place at all in my particular life. Gauguin faced the question of what place the goods of painting should have in *his* life. It may have been best for Gauguin *qua* painter that he went to

Tahiti. If it was, it does not follow that it was best for Gauguin *qua* human being or best for him *qua* father. We therefore need to distinguish between what it is that makes certain goods goods and goods to be valued for their own sake from what it is that makes it good for this particular individual or this particular society in this particular situation to make them objects of her or his or their effective practical regard. And our judgments about how it is best for an individual or a community to order the goods in their lives exemplify this third type of ascription, one whereby we judge unconditionally about what it is best for individuals or groups to be or do or have not only *qua* agents engaged in this or that form of activity in this or that role or roles, but also *qua* human beings. It is these judgments that are judgments about human flourishing.

How far human beings in particular situations need to articulate, to reflect upon and to evaluate those different types of tacit or explicit judgments about goods which furnish them with their reasons for acting varies from culture to culture and within cultures from situation to situation. But the question 'Why should I do this rather than that?' becomes from an early age inescapable and it is characteristic of human beings, that their replies to this question can themselves always be put in question, and that, when those replies are put in question, that further question can only be answered, rather than avoided or ignored, by reflecting upon and evaluating the practical reasoning that issued in or was presupposed by their actions. Human beings need to learn to understand themselves as practical reasoners about goods, about what on particular occasions it is best for them to do and about how it is best for them to live out their lives.

Without learning this human beings cannot flourish and in this respect of course they differ from dolphins, so that their vulnerability is also of a different order. Like dolphins their social relationships are indispensable to their flourishing, but what they need from their social relationships is much that is specific to human flourishing as well as much that is shared with other intelligent species. Dolphins can flourish without being able to argue with and learn from others about dolphin flourishing. Humans at times cannot flourish without arguing with others and learning from them about human flourishing. And so everything that can inhibit, frustrate or damage the exercise of the powers of reasoning is a potential threat. Toxic substances, diseases, injuries, predators, and lack of food threaten dolphins, humans, and other species equally. But the development of human beings into effective practical reasoners is threatened in additional ways.

Human infants, in the earliest stages of life after birth, like very young dolphins in the same stages, direct themselves towards the immediate satisfaction of felt bodily wants: for milk and the breast, for warmth and security, for freedom from this or that discomfort or pain, for sleep. This is our first experience of the achievement of goods and, in taking notice of it, we recognize that the threefold classification of ascriptions of good which I have elaborated is incomplete. We also and at a primary stage recognize as good and call good the pleasures attained in the satisfaction of felt bodily wants, indeed of felt wants more generally. To develop beyond this stage is to recognize not just a wider range of goods, but a wider range of kinds of good. Dolphins too develop and in the natural course of their development become directed towards different kinds of goods, goods of sociable hunting and play, for example. But, as they grow older the directedness of their activities and the objects towards which desire is directed do in some respects change, but change as part of their natural development. They do not have to go through a stage in which they separate themselves from their desires, as humans do, a separation which involves a recognition of goods other than the pleasures of satisfied bodily wants. What do I mean in saying this?

When someone gives a reason for doing this rather than that, it is never sufficient, either to explain or to justify one's action, to say "I did x, because doing x enabled me to do, have or be y and I wanted to do, have or be y." Why not? Because it is always relevant to ask why I should at this particular time in these particular circumstances choose to act on this particular desire rather than on some other. At any particular time I have some range of projects, of goals, and of desires. So, when I propose to myself to act on this particular desire, I have to ask "Is it at this time and in these circumstances best to act so as to satisfy this particular desire?" And, if I do act on a particular desire, I either make or presuppose a judgment that it is best for me here and now to act so as to satisfy this particular desire. In our everyday speech of course the explanation or justification of some particular action by an agent often does terminate with her or him saying something such as "I did it, just because that is what I wanted to do." But, if this is what I say, I always invite the question of whether there was not some better reason for me to act in some other way. Hence if my reason for acting as I did was a good reason for so acting, it must have been not just that I wanted such and such, but that I wanted such and such *and* that there was no better reason for acting in any other way.

In so evaluating my desires I stand back from them, I put some distance between them and myself *qua* practical reasoner, just because I invite the question, both from myself and from others, of whether it is in fact good for me to act on this particular desire here and now. Most of the time deliberation does proceed and must proceed without bringing this question to mind. And, if this question were raised too often and too insistently, it would paralyze us as agents. But without the ability to raise it we cannot function as practical reasoners and the acquisition of this ability is possible only for those who have to some significant degree learned how to separate themselves from their desires and more especially from those desires in their primitive, infantile forms. The small child, if possible, acts on its desires, finding in them reasons for action, as dolphins do, as gorillas do. What the use of language enables it to achieve is, as Kenny, McDowell, and others have emphasized, the evaluation of its reasons. But the acquisition of language is not by itself sufficient. The child has to learn that it may have good reason to act other than as its most urgently felt wants dictate and it can do this only when those wants have ceased to be its dictator.

It is not of course that the child becomes able to act without desire. The notion of acting without desire is itself a phantasy and a dangerous one. It is rather that the child becomes open to considerations regarding its good. It develops a desire for doing, being, and having what it is good for it to do, be, and have, and in so doing becomes motivated by reasons that direct it towards some good. Notice however that in justifying our actions and our having acted from this or that desire for this or that object we make no reference to the desire for good *qua* desire. It is always and only some claim about the character of the good in question and about why it is best for us in this particular situation to act so as to achieve this good that is relevant to such justification.

It is therefore of some importance that in our philosophical analyses we should not in general assimilate evaluations and expressions of desire. (We need, that is, an Aristotelian rather than a Davidsonian account of these matters; on Aristotle's view see Thomas M. Tuozzo, 'Conceptualized and Unconceptualized Desire in Aristotle', *Journal of the History of Philosophy* xxxii, 4, October 1994 and on Davidson's his *Expressing Evaluations*, Manhattan: University of Kansas Press, 1982.) For if we do so, we will be unable to map the progress of the young child from those earlier stages at which as yet there is for the child no distinction to be made between these to that later stage at which she or he begins to distinguish between the answers to the questions 'What do I want?' or 'What do I most want?' and the answers to the question 'What is it best for me to do?'

The child of course learns to make this distinction through encountering others who apply it to her or him, before he or she is able to apply it to her or himself, in such utterances as 'Stop eating that! I know that you like it, but it's bad for you' or 'This will hurt, but you will not get well, unless I do it.' And in learning from others how to apply this distinction to her or himself the child also has to recognize a further difference between judgments that give expression to or report our wants and judgments about what is good or best for us. Each of us is in the last analysis the authority on her or his own desires.

Knowing what we want is not always easy and we may on occasion fail to recognize what it is that we really want and need help from others in finding our way to such a recognition. But a want is something that, if I have it, I must be able to avow and often only I can avow. But I am not similarly authoritative in respect of judgments about what it is good or best for me to do or be or have.

What is or would be good or best for me is something on which, apart from the fact that generally and characteristically I know more about myself than others do, I may in many and crucial respects be no more of an authority than some others and in some respects a good deal less of an authority than some others. My physician, or my trainer, if I am an athlete, or my teacher, if I am a student, may well be better placed to make judgments about my good than I am. And so on occasion may my friends. About both goods in general and our own good in particular we have to learn from others, if we are to be able to judge truly for ourselves, and the others whom we first encounter as teachers are such persons as parents, aunts, nurses, and the like. What each of us has to do, in order to develop our powers as independent reasoners, and so to flourish *qua* members of our species, is to make the transition from accepting what we are taught by those earliest teachers to making our own independent judgments about goods, judgments that we are able to justify rationally to ourselves and to others as furnishing us with good reasons for acting in this way rather than that. This transition has a threefold character.

It begins from our infant condition as human animals, dependent as the infant dolphin or the infant gorilla are dependent. It is completed when and insofar as we emerge as independent practical reasoners. And it has at least three dimensions, two of which have already been noticed. All three of these are made possible by the possession of language, but each requires not only the ability to use language, but also an ability to put it to particular uses which require still other capacities. The first salient aspect of this transition, as I noted earlier, is that it is a movement from merely having reasons to

power analysis

being able to evaluate our reasons as good or bad reasons and by so doing to change our reasons for acting and in consequence our actions. Did we not share that initial directedness towards certain goods which is exhibited by dolphins and gorillas as well as by humans and which provides us with our initial reasons for action, there would be no starting point for this transition. And if we did not become gradually able to engage in more and more of those activities through which children and young adults learn to recognize a range of different goods we would not progress towards its completion, a progress that is always beset by obstacles, difficulties and dangers.

Any catalogue of these obstacles, difficulties, and dangers has to begin with much the same list of lethal agents that threaten dolphins: diseases, injuries, predators, malnutrition, and starvation. But to these we have to add all those other agents and conditions that threaten the development of the child's linguistic and reason-evaluating capacities: failure to provide adequate stimulus to brain activity, mental retardation, autism, anxiety-engendering insecurity, conditions that render a child unable to control its aggression, too much fear, insufficient hopefulness—and the list could go on. But it already includes enough to direct our attention to another already noticed dimension of the child's transition from dependent infancy to the agency of an independent practical reasoner, that which involves the transformation of the child's desires and passions.

To have learned how to stand back in some measure from our present desires, so as to be able to evaluate them, is a necessary condition for engaging in sound reasoning about our reasons for action. Here one danger is that those who have failed to become sufficiently detached from their own immediate desires, for whom desire for their and the good has not become to a sufficient degree overriding, are unlikely to recognize this fact about themselves. And so what they present to themselves as a desire for their own good or for *the* good may in fact be and often enough is some unacknowledged form of infantile desire, a type of desire that has been protected from evaluative criticism. Hence in deliberating they both reason from unsound premises and act from badly flawed motivation. Sound practical reasoning and good motivation are related in sometimes complex ways, but an incapacity to distance oneself from one's desires is a danger to both.

The history of any self making this transition is of course not only a history of that particular self, but also a history of those particular others whose presence or absence, intervention or lack of intervention, are of crucial importance in determining how far the transition is successfully completed. And those others enter into that history in two different ways. They provide first of all the resources for making the transition, by nursing, feeding, clothing, nurturing, teaching, restraining, and advising. What resources an individual needs varies with circumstances, temperament, and above all the obstacles and difficulties that have to be confronted. We need others to help us avoid encountering and falling victim to disabling conditions, but when, often inescapably, we do fall victim, either temporarily or permanently, to such conditions as those of blindness, deafness, crippling injury, debilitating disease, or psychological disorder, we need others to sustain us, to help us in obtaining needed, often scarce, resources, to help us discover what new ways forward there may be, and to stand in our place from time to time, doing on our behalf what we cannot do for ourselves. Different individuals, disabled in different ways and degrees, can have their own peculiar talents and possibilities, and their own difficulties. Each therefore needs others to take note of her or his particular condition. And this is one of the points at which it is important to remember that there is a scale of disability on which we all find ourselves. Disability is a matter of more or less, both in respect of degree of disability and in respect of the time periods in which we are disabled. And at different periods of our lives we find ourselves, often unpredictably, at very different points on that scale. When we pass from one such point to another we need others to recognize that we remain the same individuals that we were before making this or that transition. Yet the part that others play in assisting us to make such transitions is far from the only way in which they figure in our history.

The very young child from the moment of birth and indeed even before that is engaged in and defined by a set of social relationships which are not at all of her or his own making. The passage that the child has to make is to a condition in which her or his social relationships are those of one independent practical reasoner to other independent practical reasoners as well as to those who in turn at some later stage become dependent on her or him. Independent practical reasoners contribute to the formation and sustaining of their social relationships, as infants do not, and to learn how to become an independent practical reasoner is to learn how to cooperate with others in forming and sustaining those same relationships that make possible the achievement of common goods by independent practical reasoners. Such cooperative activities presuppose some degree of shared understanding of present and future possibilities.

The movement from awareness only of the present to awareness informed by an imagined future is a third dimension of the transition from infancy to the condition of an independent practical reasoner. This too, like the ability to evaluate our reasons for action and the ability to distance ourselves from our present desires, is an ability that requires both the possession of language and the capacity to put language to a wide range of different uses. Members of non-language-using intelligent species cannot possess it. Wittgenstein said: "One can imagine an animal (*Tier*) angry, frightened, unhappy, happy, startled. But hopeful? And why not?" And he goes on to point out that a dog may believe that its master is at the door, but not that its master will come the day after tomorrow (*Philosophical Investigations* II, i, 174).

How we structure our understanding of the future depends in part of course on the established uses of clocks, calendars, and modes of scheduling of the culture in which we find ourselves. But as a practical reasoner I have to be able to imagine different possible futures *for me*, to imagine myself moving forward from the starting point of the present in different directions. For different or alternative futures present me with different and alternative sets of goods to be achieved, with different possible modes of flourishing. And it is important that I should be able to envisage both nearer and more distant futures and to attach probabilities, even if only in a rough and ready way, to the future results of acting in one way rather than another. For this both knowledge and imagination are necessary.

As with the other abilities and capacities that we need, the development of the required kind of imagination is vulnerable to a range of threatening contingencies, and not only those already catalogued. Children can be provided with too constrained and impoverished a view of future possibilities. And this can happen to any child. But it is a kind of harm to which those already afflicted with some measure of disability may be peculiarly liable. For it is and perhaps always has been a common assumption that blindness, deafness, deformed or injured limbs, and the like exclude the sufferer from more than a very, very limited set of possibilities. And this has often been treated as if it were a fact of nature. What is thereby obscured is the extent to which whether and how far the obstacles presented by those afflictions can be overcome or circumvented depends not only on the resources of the disabled—and these will vary a great deal from individual to individual—but also on what others contribute, others whose failures may be failures of imagination with respect to future possibilities. What disability amounts to, that is, depends not just on the disabled individual, but on the groups of which that individual is a member.

It is not only however of the disabled that this is true. Others too may become the victims of an inability to imagine alternative realistic futures, because in some crucial stages of early life they were not provided with enough of an education in imagining alternative possibilities. Educational failure in this respect can be of two contrasting kinds. On the one hand, as with the disabled, it can produce a constriction of the sense of possibility through the inculcation of false beliefs about how far our lives are determined by uncontrollable circumstances. On the other it can encourage a giving way to self-indulgent phantasy which blurs the difference between realistic expectations and wishful thinking. And either of these will render us defective practical reasoners. The latter type of failure prevents us from recognizing the limits upon our choices; the former prevents us from recognizing how many and how varied are the alternatives between which we can choose. Both types of failure generally involve an inadequate understanding of the parts that others do play and can play in our lives, both in enlarging and in diminishing possibility.

This third dimension in the transition from dependent infancy to the independence of practical reasoners is closely bound up with the other two. When someone asks if what they have taken to be a good reason for doing such and such is a sufficiently good reason, it is usually necessary for them to enquire what else it is that they might have done or be doing, what the alternative future possibilities were or are. So too learning how to detach oneself from one's immediate desires, so as to be able to ask 'Is it good and best to act here and now so as to satisfy this or that particular desire?' requires understanding what range of objects of desire and what range of goods are presented by alternative futures. We have to learn to understand ourselves as directed to a range of goals that are more or less remote from our present situation and to order our desires accordingly.

The relationship between the three dimensions is complex. But they all contribute to a single process of development and a significant degree of failure in any one of the three areas will be liable to produce or reinforce significant failure in the others. As it is with learners, so also it is with teachers: to be defective as a teacher in any one area may be a cause of being defective in all three. When I speak of teachers here, I mean of course all those, and especially the parents, who care for, interact with and teach young children as they reach the point where specifically human modes of flourishing become open to them. When I speak of independent practical reasoning, I refer to the exercise of human powers of rationality in very different types of culture and economy and therefore in very different contexts of practice: hunting, farming, mercantile, industrial. What it is for human beings to flourish does of course vary from context to context, but in every context it is as someone exercises in a relevant way the capacities of an independent practical reasoner that her or his potentialities for flourishing in a specifically human way are developed. So if we want to understand how it is good for humans to live, we need to know what it is to be excellent as an independent practical reasoner, that is, what the virtues of independent practical reasoning are. But we need to know more than this.

Because of the part that others play in enabling us to move from the condition of infancy to that of an independent practical reasoner, we also need to know what it is for those others to perform *their* part excellently, what the virtues of caring and teaching are and how they relate to the virtues of the practical reasoner. So having raised the question of what specifically human flourishing consists in, we find almost immediately, just as Aristotle did, that it has become the question of what the virtues are and of what it is to live the kind of life that the exercise of the virtues requires. It will be retorted that this is scarcely surprising. If one begins by posing one's questions in Aristotelian terms, as I have done, then naturally enough, the attempt to formulate answers to them will develop along Aristotelian lines. But to begin as I did is, it will be said, question-begging. It is to take for granted rather than to show that some version of Aristotelianism is superior to other relevant philosophical standpoints. And this charge must be conceded. But in conceding it two kinds of remark need to be made.

The first is that every starting point for philosophical enquiry is initially question-begging in just this way. There is no presuppositionless point of departure. What vindicates this or that starting point is what comes next, the enquiry thus generated and its outcome in the achievement of some particular kind of understanding of some subject matter. One mark of adequate understanding is that it explains retrospectively why enquiry well-designed to achieve it could have begun from some types of starting point, but not from others. It is only by arriving at an adequate formulation of the relevant set of first principles in the end that our initial assumptions and procedures are vindicated.

Yet to this it may well be said that I have merely provided further grounds for the accusation, since to a more or less Aristotelian starting point I have now added a more or less Aristotelian conception of how the enquiry is to proceed. And this again I must concede: there is a good deal of further philosophical work to be done, which I shall not be doing here. And this is especially the case in one particular area.

Earlier I catalogued a variety of types of ascription of good, of uses of 'good' and of its cognates. That catalogue takes as the focal uses of 'good' those in which it ascribes directly or indirectly flourishing to members of some plant or animal species *qua* members of that species. And these focal uses provide the underlying unity in terms of which the multiplicity of types of ascription of good is to be explained. Since I have taken it to be a question of fact, albeit sometimes in particular respects a disputed matter, what it is for members of this or that particular species to flourish, I am committed to giving what is in some sense a naturalistic account of good and of 'good', since insofar as a plant or animal is flourishing, it is so in virtue of possessing some relevant set of natural characteristics. But to say this is not of course to say that the meaning of 'good' can be given by constructing some list of natural characteristics, even by some very long disjunctive list, and to say that good is a property that supervenes upon some set of natural characteristics is to give a name to the problem of how to understand the relationship between goodness and such characteristics, not to solve it.

Notorious and difficult philosophical problems arise in this area and here I put them on one side. I notice only that even to catalogue the uses of 'good' in this way seems to render certain types of philosophical theory about 'good' *prima facie* implausible. Whatever it means to say of some particular member of some particular species that it is flourishing, that it is achieving its good, or that this or that is good for it, in that it conduces to its flourishing—assertions that we can make about thistles and cabbages, donkeys and dolphins, in the same sense of 'flourishing' and the same sense of 'good'—it is difficult to suppose either that in making such assertions we are ascribing some nonnatural property or that we are expressing an attitude, an emotion, or an endorsement.

8

How do we become independent practical reasoners?
How do the virtues make this possible?

What then are the social relationships without which we cannot become independent practical reasoners? Are there also social relationships that are necessary if we are to be sustained as independent practical reasoners? And what are the virtues without which these relationships cannot be brought into being and maintained in being? If we are to answer these questions, we first need a further and more detailed account of the dimensions of the child's development out of infantile dependence.

In most moral philosophy the starting point is one that already presupposes the existence of mature independent practical reasoners whose social relationships are the relationships of the adult world. Childhood, if noticed at all, is a topic that receives only brief and incidental attention. (There are of course a very few but striking exceptions, among them Rousseau's

Émile and more recently Gareth B. Matthews's *The Philosophy of Childhood*, Cambridge, Mass.: Harvard University Press, 1994. The neglect of childhood parallels the neglect both of old age and of experiences, at all stages of life, of disability and dependence.) But practical reasoners enter the adult world with relationships, experiences, attitudes, and capacities that they bring with them from childhood and adolescence and that always to some significant, and often to some very large degree they are unable to discard and disown.

To become an effective independent practical reasoner is an achievement, but it is always one to which others have made essential contributions. The earliest of these relate directly to our animal existence, to what we share in our development with members of other intelligent species. We owe to parents, especially mothers, to aunts, grandparents, and surrogates for these, that care from conception through birth and infancy to childhood that dolphins also owe to elders who provide maternal and other care. And in human as in dolphin life there are patterns of receiving and giving, enduring through and beyond the life-span of particular individuals. Dolphins, having been cared for, care for others, sometimes extending such care beyond their own species to human beings. So Plutarch, in a dialogue comparing the excellences of sea creatures to those of land animals, ascribed to dolphins—in contrast to what he took to be the narrow self-interest of swallows—"that virtue so much sought after by the best philosophers: the capacity for disinterested friendship" (*Moralia* LXIII, 'Whether Land or Sea Animals Have More Practical Intelligence'). But, tempting as this thought about dolphins may be, it emphasizes a resemblance at the cost of obscuring a difference.

The care for others that dolphins exhibit plays a crucial part in sustaining their shared lives. Yet this part is one that they themselves cannot survey, lacking as they do, any capacity to look back to infancy or forward to aging and death as humans do. Both dolphins and humans have animal identities and animal histories. Human beings are able on occasion to ignore or to conceal from themselves this fact, perhaps by thinking of themselves instead as Lockean persons or Cartesian minds or even as Platonic souls (See for a statement of some of the relevant philosophical issues and arguments Eric T. Olson, *The Human Animal: Personal Identity without Psychology* Oxford: Oxford University Press, 1998). But, unlike dolphins, they also have the possibility of understanding their animal identity through time from conception to death and with it their need at different past and future stages of life for the care of others, that is, as those who, having received care, will be from time to time called upon to give care, and who, having given, will from time to time themselves once more be in need of care by and from others. What we need from others, if we are not only to exercise our initial animal capacities, but also to develop the capacities of independent practical reasoners, are those relationships necessary for fostering the ability to evaluate, modify, or reject our own practical judgments, to ask, that is, whether what we take to be good reasons for action really are sufficiently good reasons, *and* the ability to imagine realistically alternative possible futures, so as to be able to make rational choices between them, *and* the ability to stand back from our desires, so as to be able to enquire rationally what the pursuit of our good here and now requires and how our desires must be directed and, if necessary, reeducated, if we are to attain it. It is the last of these that we should consider first.

I have already remarked that one early cause of inadequacy as a practical reasoner is a failure to separate ourselves adequately from our desires, so as to be able, when necessary, to pass judgment on those desires from an external point of view. This incapacity, I have suggested, characteristically results from a failure to make ourselves sufficiently independent of those others on whom we depended, first for sustenance during infancy and then for initiating us into the procedures of practical reasoning. For it is not just that the infant desires immediate satisfaction of clamorous felt needs. It is also that those desires become focused upon whomsoever and whatever it is that satisfies those needs. And the attitudes of the child towards the objects of its desires are informed by attachments and affections—and accompanying deprivations, pains, and fears—that for it define its first social relationships.

All this may seem too obvious to be worth remarking. But it provides reminders that are badly needed if we are to understand the full extent of the difficulty confronted by parents and others whose aim is to enable dependent young children to become independent reasoners, practical reasoners who not only have the ability to reach their own conclusions, but also can be held accountable by and to others for those conclusions. The resources that they bring to this task derive largely from the child's initial dependence. The child will have learned through its experiences of attachment and affection that, in order to satisfy its desires, it must please its mother and other adult figures. It therefore acts so as to please those adults. Yet what those adults have to teach the child, if the child is indeed to become an independent practical reasoner, is that it will please them, *not* by acting so as to please them, but by acting so as to achieve what is good and best, whether this pleases them or not. All adults find it difficult and some find it impossible to teach this. So that the early learning of the child is characteristically imperfect learning at the hands of imperfect teachers, in which the child confronts conflicting demands and responds, if her or his teachers are successful, in struggling against this imposition. The imperfection of the teacher, we should note, is a matter not only of the difficulty of the task, but also of the fact that the teacher too was once an imperfect learner.

The child who has become adequately independent both of her or his own desires and of the undue influence of adults will therefore generally have had to free her or himself through a series of conflicts. How to engage in conflict, so that one is destructive neither to oneself nor to others, is another skill that has to be learned early and it too is generally learned imperfectly. We are therefore never completely weaned from either the attachments or the antagonisms characteristic of early childhood, nor is it perhaps desirable that we should be. But what we should have learned from reflection upon the practice of psychoanalysis, and most of all perhaps from the work of

D. W. Winnicott, is that one outcome of failure to transform the attitudes and relationships of early childhood is an inability to achieve the kind of independence that is able to acknowledge truthfully and realistically its dependences and attachments, so leaving us in captivity to those dependences, attachments, and conflicts. Acknowledgment of dependence is the key to independence. For one consequence of failure to break free from such captivity may be an inability even to acquire an adequate sense of oneself as an independent person with one's own unity as an agent. Winnicott has shown us how in achieving this sense of self there is a sequence in which "relaxation in conditions of trust based on experience" is followed by "creative, physical and mental activity manifested in play," so that finally there is a "summation of these experiences forming the basis for a sense of self" (*Playing and Reality*, London: Tavistock, 1971, p. 56). (Winnicott in the passage from which I am quoting uses this sequence to narrate the history of an analysis, but it also has application to the histories of early childhood.) Play is important because it is exploratory, because it releases those who engage in it from the pressures of felt need, because it extends both the range of activities found worth pursuing for their own sake and the range of pleasures that can be taken in such activities, and because in moving from the kind of playfulness exhibited both by humans and dolphins to more sophisticated forms of play we move from animal intelligence to specifically human reasoning (see D. W. Winnicott, 'The Baby as a Person', chapter 11 of *The Child, the Family, and the Outside World*, Reading, Mass.: Addison-Wesley, 1987). What analysts are sometimes able to provide for those whose early childhood experiences were defective is what good mothers and other caregiving adults do provide, a situation in which the child's unqualified trust in such adults releases the creative physical and mental powers expressed in play, resulting in a sense of self sufficient for an increasing degree of independence in practical reasoning.

What I become able to do, if I acquire an adequate sense of self, is to put in question the relationship between my present

set of desires and motives and my good. What constitutes a
good reason for my doing this rather than that, for my acting
from this particular desire rather than that, is that my doing this
rather than that serves my good, will contribute to my flourishing *qua* human being. But what if my desires are otherwise
directed? Very young children initially cannot but pursue the
satisfaction of their wants and felt needs without any reference
to a good beyond that satisfaction. And with adults it is often
the case in particular situations that what it would be good and
best for them to do is one thing, while what they want to do is
quite another. In the case of both children and adults there is a
gap between what they have good reason to do and what would
satisfy some present desire or other member of what Bernard
Williams has called "the agent's subjective motivational set"
('Internal and External Reasons', *Moral Luck*, Cambridge:
Cambridge University Press, 1981, p. 102), defining this
broadly so that it includes "dispositions of evaluation, patterns
of emotional reaction, personal loyalties" and commitments to
various projects (p. 105).

Williams has argued that there can be no such thing as a
reason for action by a particular agent which is external to and
independent of the members of this agent's motivational set,
but he is careful to point out that we should not think of that
set as "statically given" (p. 105). So Williams certainly allows
that an agent may come to be moved by considerations which
do not at present move her or him; what had been an external
reason may become an internal reason. But what Williams's
conclusion does exclude is the possibility that it can be true of
some particular agent that it would be good and best for her or
him *qua* human being or *qua* aunt or *qua* farmer to do such and
such, and that *therefore* she or he has good reason to do such
and such, independently of whether or not at any present or
future time that agent will have, perhaps even could have, given
her or his individual circumstances, the requisite motivation.
And it seems that this is because for Williams to assert about
some agent that it would be good and best for her or him to do
such and such is one thing, while to assert about that same

agent that she or he has reason to do such and such is quite another. Williams's account certainly allows for moral development of some kinds, but it obscures from view the way in which agents have to learn at various stages how to transcend what have been up till this or that point the limitations of their motivational set and will fail badly in their moral development, if they remain within those limitations.

What a child who is making the transition from the infantile exercise of animal intelligence to the exercise of independent practical reasoning has to achieve is a transformation of her or his motivational set, so that what were originally—in Williams' terminology, although now differently understood—external reasons also become internal. This is the passage from desiring x and wanting my desire for x to be satisfied, just because it is my desire, to desiring x qua good and wanting my desire for x to be satisfied, just because and insofar as it is a desire for what it is good and best for me to desire. What are the qualities that a child must develop, first to redirect and transform her or his desires, and subsequently to direct them consistently towards the goods of the different stages of her or his life? They are the intellectual and moral virtues. It is because failure to acquire those virtues makes it impossible for us to achieve this transition that the virtues have the place and function that they do in human life. How do they enable us to do this? Even a minimally adequate answer must wait upon a more extended account of the transition through which the child must pass and of its end-state. But enough has already been said to make it clear that certain kinds of answer are ruled out.

Just because our degree of success or failure in first acquiring and then practicing the virtues determines in significant measure what it is that we find agreeable and useful, the characterization of the virtues, in Humean terms, as qualities that are generally and naturally agreeable and useful is misleading. Consider the virtue of temperateness, the virtue concerned with the pleasures and pains of eating, drinking, sexuality, and other bodily activities and states. To have this virtue is not only to know how to avoid the extremes of self-indulgent and even addictive appetite, on the one hand, and of an unappreciative and insensitive puritanism on the other, but also to do so, as Aristotle remarked, with an eye to our own particular circumstances. What temperateness requires of an athlete in training is not what it requires of a convalescent whose strength needs to be rebuilt. What it requires of someone who is tempted to excess in eating is not the same as what it requires of someone whose vice is fanatical devotion to a cult of fitness and weight-loss.

Someone who has become temperate will have come to enjoy moderation and to find excess disagreeable and even painful. She or he will no longer practice moderation in spite of a desire for the pleasures that belong to excess, but because desire itself has been transformed. What she or he finds agreeable and useful is no longer the same. And temperateness itself will now have become agreeable and will now be recognized as useful. The class of the virtues, that is to say, includes some virtues at least, such as temperateness, that are agreeable to and are recognized as useful by those who possess them, but that may well seem disagreeable and even harmful not only to those with the corresponding vices, but also to those whose purposes are such that it is useful to them that others should have those vices. So it is highly agreeable and useful to those who market certain kinds of consumer goods that there should be intemperate consumers. Their own vice of acquisitiveness makes the vice of intemperateness in others agreeable and useful to them.

The progress of the child towards a condition in which she or he is able to stand back from her or his desires and evaluate them is then in key part an extended initiation into those habits that are the virtues. And the child's teachers will need themselves in some measure to possess those virtues, if they are to be able to instruct the child. But we would make a mistake, if we inferred from this that some part of the child's education has to be set apart for specifically moral instruction. Just as the virtues are exercised in the whole range of our activities, so they are learned in the same range of activities, in those contexts of practice in which we learn from others how to discharge our roles and functions first as members of a family and household, then in the tasks of schoolwork, and later on as farmworkers or carpenters or teachers or members of a fishing crew or a string quartet. For to be instructed in the virtues together with the relevant skills is nothing other than to learn how to discharge those roles and functions well rather than badly. (There is of course a good deal to be said about the content of an education that directs those who receive it towards the virtues and the content of an education that does not. It will not be said here.)

Teachers in general then—parents, other family members, those who instruct apprentices in crafts—have to have in significant measure the habits that they try to inculcate. But they also need other virtues and what these are varies with the type of teaching that their role requires. All teaching requires some degree of care for the student *qua* student as well as for the subject matter of the teaching. But there are kinds of teaching—the teaching of piano or violin, for example—in which the ruthless exclusion of the talentless from further teaching (a mercy to the student as well as to the teacher and to any innocent bystanders) is one of the marks of a good teacher and in which the abilities to identify the talentless and to exclude them are among her or his virtues. But with those whose care for the young child begins from birth—and in the case especially of the mother from soon after conception—the care that becomes instructive has to be of quite another order with some quite other virtues. Indeed the care that the very young child needs from its mother, the care given by what Winnicott called "the ordinary good mother" (*Home Is Where We Start From: Essays by a Psychoanalyst*, London: Pelican Books, 1987, p. 123) may seem to be so different from its later education into the activities of various practices that it may appear odd to treat the mother's role at this stage as that of an educator. But she *is* an educator and the quality of her care is crucial for the child's later development as a learner. What then does the child learn from her at this earlier period?

The ordinary good mother provides the child with a setting

in which the child is secure enough to test out, often destructively, what can be relied upon in its experience and what cannot. In so doing the child becomes self-aware, aware of itself as the object of recognition by a mother who is responsive to its needs, who is resilient and nonretaliating in the face of its destructiveness, rather than insisting that the child adapt to her. The child who is compelled by the combination of its own needs and its mother's unresponsive attitudes to comply with the requirements of its mother becomes unable to acquire an adequate sense either of external reality or of its self. It is deprived of what it needs to become someone who adequately distinguishes between fantasy and reality ('Primary Maternal Preoccupation' in *Collected Papers: Through Paediatrics to Psychoanalysis*, London: Tavistock Press, 1958, and 'Ego Distortion in Terms of True and False Self' in *The Maturational Process and the Facilitating Environment: Studies in the Theory of Emotional Development*, London: Hogarth Press, 1965). And this distinction is one of the foundations of later learning.

What virtues must a mother have, what virtues must fathers and other family members also have, to provide the right kind of security and the right kind of responsive recognition? Parents stand in a different relationship to their own children from that of other teachers to those who learn from them and this in three ways. If parents, especially mothers, are to provide children with the security and recognition that they need, they have to make the object of their continuing care and their commitment *this* child, just because it is their child for whom and to whom they are uniquely responsible. Secondly, their initial commitment has to be in important respects unconditional. The parental, especially the maternal attitude, has to give expression to a pledge of the form: 'However things turn out, I will be there for you.' And thirdly, although it is the fact that it is their child that makes *this* child their responsibility, it is the needs of the child, and not their own needs in relationship to the child that have to be paramount. And all three aspects of the relationship involve a systematic refusal to treat the child in a way that is proportional to its qualities and aptitudes.

Before the birth of a child parents generally want that child to conform more or less to some ideal, the details of which vary from culture to culture. So characteristically they will want a child who is good-looking rather than ugly, healthy, even athletic, rather than sickly or crippled, with normal, even outstanding intellectual development, rather than with slower or retarded development, and the like. But the commitment to care of the ordinary good parent to this or that particular child, if the parent is to provide the security and recognition needed by the child, has to be a commitment to care for the child, even if it turns out to be ugly, sickly, and retarded. And this holds for good parents of normally developing, healthy, intelligent, and good-looking children just as much as for parents of children who suffer disfigurement or brain damage. Good parental care is defined in part by reference to the possibility of the affliction of their children by serious disability. The parents of children who are in fact severely disabled do of course sometimes need to be heroic in their exercise of the relevant virtues as the parents of ordinary children do not. They have undertaken one of the most demanding kinds of work that there is. But it is the parents of the seriously disabled who are the paradigms of good motherhood and fatherhood as such, who provide the model for and the key to the work of all parents.

What those who perform the role and function of a good parent achieve is to bring the child to the point at which it is educable, not only by them but also by a variety of other different kinds of teacher. And this is the first step towards making the child independent as a reasoner. For what the child has had to learn in order to be so educable is how to stand back from its own desires and how to ask if this or that particular desire is one which it is best for it to satisfy here and now and so the child moves beyond its initial animal state of *having reasons for acting in this way rather than that* towards its specifically human state of *being able to evaluate those reasons, to revise them or to abandon them and replace them with others*. And now the child's dependence is of a new kind.

That new dependence, as I have already noted, is upon those

who have the task of teaching children and young adults the elements of various practices, something that involves not only the acquisition of skills, but also the recognition of the goods internal to each practice, those goods in terms of whose achievement excellence in this or that particular practice is defined. Those qualities of mind and character that enable someone both to recognize the relevant goods and to use the relevant skills in achieving them are the excellences, the virtues, that distinguish or should distinguish teacher from apprentice or student. Such virtues can be characterized in two different but closely related ways. They are on the one hand qualities exhibited in responsiveness to different kinds of situation: knowing when to take risks and when to be cautious, when to delegate a task to others and when to take it on oneself, when to be generous with deserved praise and sparing of deserved blame, when to be exacting whether with oneself or with others and when to be more relaxed, when a joke is needed and when anger is appropriate. As such, those qualities are familiar to us in conventional catalogues of the virtues: the risk-taking and patience of courage, justice in assigning tasks and praise, the temperateness required for discipline, the cheerful wit of an amiable will. But these same virtues can also be characterized as qualities exhibited—or not exhibited—in an agent's practical reasoning.

The conclusion of sound and effective practical reasoning is an action, that action which it is best for this particular agent to do in these particular circumstances. Reasoning that issues in action has to begin with premises about the goods that are at stake in some particular situation and the harms and dangers that threaten their achievement. But to recognize in one's practice what goods are at stake in this or that particular situation and what the threats to them are and to find in those goods premises for an argument whose conclusion will be a just action is to exhibit the kind of responsiveness that characterizes the virtues. At some later stage there will be situations in which the further question may arise of whether what the child or the young adult has hitherto taken to be good, on the basis of her or his earlier learning, really is good and really is the good that it is best to set oneself to achieve here and now in this particular situation. And to answer such questions there will have to be further reasoning. But initially what the child needs to learn is *how* to recognize the salient features of each situation immediately, what the relevant goods, harms, and dangers are in each situation, and what the virtues require by way of response.

It is in learning how to respond that children learn how to employ discriminatingly those different uses of 'good' and of its cognates that I have already catalogued. They learn—or fail to learn—in a variety of contexts of practice to judge truly that it is good to do *this*, because doing this is the best means available for bringing about *that*. They learn—or fail to learn—to judge that it is unqualifiedly good in such and such a range of circumstances to bring about *that*. And they learn—or fail to learn—that, out of the range of goods that they might set themselves to achieve here and now *that* is the good which it is best for them here and now to achieve.

Rule-following will often be involved in knowing how to respond rightly, but no rule or set of rules by itself ever determines how to respond rightly. This is because in the case of those rules that are always to be respected—'Never take an innocent life', for example—they are never sufficient to determine how we ought to act, while with other rules what always has to be determined is whether in this particular case they are relevant and, if so, how they are to be applied. And there is no higher order rule by reference to which these questions can be universally answered. Children very early on have to learn, for example, how to behave, when strangers appear. So someone may have to ask: Is this a case for obeying the rule that prescribes offering hospitality to strangers? Or is it rather a case for obeying the rule that prescribes treating those who are potentially dangerous with wariness and suspicion? Neither kind of rule, neither inviolable negative rules nor positive prescriptions, can by itself be a sufficient guide to action. Knowing how to act virtuously always involves more than rule-following.

Practical reasoning, as I noticed earlier, has still further dimensions and those who are to engage in it adequately require skills as well as virtues and self-knowledge as well as both (although we may well want to count self-knowledge among the virtues). For without these they will be unable to imagine that range of alternative possible futures that are, given their social circumstances and their own characteristics, futures that it would be realistic for them to attempt to make their own. So they need relevant knowledge of both the particularities of those parts of the natural and social world which impinge upon them and of those generalizations which will enable them to judge the probability of different outcomes of this or that kind of action in this or that kind of situation. And they will also need self-knowledge concerning their own physical abilities, temperaments, character, and skills. For the greater part of our knowledge of the natural and social world we of course have to rely upon what others—the majority of them others of whom we have no first-hand knowledge—have communicated to us, in order to supplement the meagerness of our individual experience. But our self-knowledge too depends in key part upon what we learn about ourselves from others, and more than this, upon a confirmation of our own judgments about ourselves by others who know us well, a confirmation that only such others can provide.

We have been reminded by a number of philosophers influenced by Wittgenstein that human identity has an inescapably double aspect. When I remember that I succeeded or failed in doing so and so, and, in the act of remembering, judge or presuppose that I am the selfsame human being here and now who did or failed to do so and so then and there, I do not rely upon criteria. And it makes no sense to ask me *how* I know that I am the same human being who did or failed to do so and so. But when others judge that I here and now am one and the same human being whom they remember doing or failing to do so and so then and there, their judgments are and cannot but be criterion-grounded. And it makes unproblematic sense to ask them how they know that I am the same human being who did or failed to do so and so. It is only because criterionless ungrounded self-ascriptions of identity coincide in the overwhelming majority of cases with the criterion-grounded ascriptions of identity by others that we are able to have the concept of human identity that we do. And it is only because of this coincidence of judgments that each of us is able to treat our own self-ascriptions as generally reliable. I can be said truly to know who and what I am, only because there are others who can be said truly to know who and what I am.

Unsurprisingly self-knowledge has this same double aspect—unsurprisingly, because our self-knowledge both presupposes and is presupposed by our self-ascriptions of identity. It is because and insofar as my judgments about myself agree with the judgments about me made by others who know me well that I can generally have confidence in them. And it is insofar as I am overprotective of myself in resisting disclosure to just such others that I am liable to become a victim of my phantasies. There are of course certain kinds of social interaction and relationship that, far from preventing imprisonment by self-deceiving phantasy, produce or reinforce it. But genuine and extensive self-knowledge becomes possible only in consequence of those social relationships which on occasion provide badly needed correction for our own judgments. When adequate self-knowledge is achieved, it is always a shared achievement. And, because adequate self-knowledge is necessary, if I am to imagine realistically the alternative futures between which I must choose, the quality of my imagination also depends in part on the contributions of others.

The virtue that is indispensable for achieving both the required degree of self-knowledge and the ability to resist all those influences that make for self-deception is of course honesty, primarily truthfulness about ourselves, both to ourselves and to others. That virtue is exercised not only in self-examination, but in accountability to those particular others who have reason to look to us to help in meeting their needs, by acknowledging to them our inadequacies and failures, wherever it is relevant to do so. So this virtue too is required if we are to become independent practical reasoners. And at this point it is perhaps worth summarizing what has been said so far about the virtues. I first of all noted that part of what is distinctive about human reasons for action, as compared with dolphin or gorilla reasons, is that we are able to evaluate our reasons as better or worse, and I then catalogued some characteristics that are necessary for those who, by exercising this ability, become sound practical reasoners, their ability to detach themselves from the immediacy of their own desires, their capacity to imagine alternative realistic futures, and their disposition to recognize and to make true practical judgments concerning a variety of kinds of good. Each of these is, so I claimed, possible only for those who have acquired a certain range of intellectual and moral virtues. We need those virtues, if we are to become independent practical reasoners, able to make up our own minds on the choices that confront us. But the acquisition of the necessary virtues, skills, and self-knowledge is something that we in key part owe to those particular others on whom we have had to depend. When we finally have become independent reasoners, generally early in our adult lives, many of these relationships of dependence are of course over. Yet this is not true of all of them. For we continue to the end of our lives to need others to sustain us in our practical reasoning. Why so?

We may at any point go astray in our practical reasoning because of intellectual error: perhaps we happen to be insufficiently well-informed about the particulars of our situation; or we have gone beyond the evidence in a way that has misled us; or we have relied too heavily on some unsubstantiated generalization. But we may also go astray because of moral error: we have been over-influenced by our dislike of someone; we have projected on to a situation some phantasy in whose grip we are; we are insufficiently sensitive to someone else's suffering. And our intellectual errors are often, although not always, rooted in our moral errors. From both types of mistake the best protections are friendship and collegiality.

In the context of particular practices we generally have no one else to rely on but those who are our expert coworkers, to make us aware both of our particular mistakes in this or that practical activity and of the sources of those mistakes in our failures in respect of virtues and skills. Outside of such contexts of practice we have to rely on our friends, including family members, for similar correction. When we are unable to rely on coworkers and friends, then our confidence in our own judgments may always become a source of illusion. And in order to be effective practical reasoners we do need to have justified confidence in our conclusions. That we generally and characteristically continue to be dependent on others in our practical reasoning does not mean that we should not from time to time defend and act upon conclusions that are at variance with the judgments of everyone else, including those on whose concurrence we normally rely most. Independence of mind requires this. But we always require exceptionally good reasons for so doing.

There is no point then in our development towards and in our exercise of independent practical reasoning at which we cease altogether to be dependent on particular others. But of course it may always happen that those on whom we depend may lack the virtues necessary for developing or sustaining our practical reasoning and so by neglect, by well-intended, but harmful misdirection, by manipulation or exploitation or victimization, may fail to prevent otherwise avoidable disability or may themselves be the active causes of disability, even on occasion intentionally, and so of defective development. (I am not losing sight of the fact that much disability is unavoidable.) Dolphins do not have reason to fear dolphins, as humans have reason to fear humans.

We have so far then identified two crucial respects in which the virtues are indispensable to human flourishing: without developing some range of intellectual and moral virtues we cannot first achieve and then continue in the exercise of practical reasoning; and without having developed some range of those same virtues we cannot adequately care for and educate others so that they first achieve and are then sustained in the exercise of practical reasoning. But now we encounter a third:

without the virtues we cannot adequately protect ourselves and each other against neglect, defective sympathies, stupidity, acquisitiveness, and malice. But in order to understand how the virtues have this threefold function we need first to characterize more fully both the kind of ordered social relationships which the exercise of the virtues requires and the importance of some particular virtues that do not always receive their due in conventional accounts of the virtues.

9

Social relationships, practical reasoning, common goods, and individual goods

We become independent practical reasoners through participation in a set of relationships to certain particular others who are able to give us what we need. When we have become independent practical reasoners, we will often, although not perhaps always, also have acquired what we need, if we are to be able to give to those others who are now in need of what formerly we needed. We find ourselves placed at some particular point within a network of relationships of giving and receiving in which, generally and characteristically, what and how far we are able to give depends in part on what and how far we received.

Consider how these relationships extend in time from conception to death, presupposing a conception of human identity as animal identity. We receive from parents and other family elders, from teachers and those to whom we are apprenticed, and from those who care for us when we are sick, injured, weakened by aging, or otherwise incapacitated. Later on others, children, students, those who are in various ways incapacitated, and others in gross and urgent need have to rely on us to give. Sometimes those others who rely on us are the same individuals from whom we ourselves received. But often enough it is from one set of individuals that we receive and to and by another that we are called on to give. So understood, the relationships from which the independent practical reasoner emerges and through which she or he continues to be sustained are such that from the outset she or he is in debt. Moreover the repayment of the debts in question is not and cannot be a matter of strict reciprocity, and not only because those to whom one is called upon to give are very often not the same individuals as those from whom one received. Even when what we receive is the same kind of care or assistance as that which we are called upon to give, it may be that one of these is far greater and more demanding than the other. And often enough what we receive and what we give are incommensurable: there is generally, for example, no relevant way of comparing what our parents gave us by way of care and education with what we are called upon to give to the same parents by way of care in illness or old age (although this account of moral relationships is in important respects at odds with that defended by Lawrence J. Becker in *Reciprocity*, London: Routledge & Kegan Paul, 1986, I have learned a good deal from it).

This is not the only asymmetry. We know from whom it is that we have received and therefore to whom we are in debt. But often we do not know to whom it is that we will be called upon to give: our parents and teachers perhaps, if they survive; our children, if we have children; those whom contingency and chance put into our care. And we do not know just what they will need. We can set in advance no limit to those possible needs, just as those who cared for us could at an earlier time have set no limits to what our needs might have been. We might have been disabled by, say, brain damage suffered at birth, or severe autism, so that those who cared for us would have found it impossible to develop the potentialities that we originally had. And the kind of care that was needed to make us what we have in fact become, independent practical reasoners, had to be, if it was to be effective, unconditional care for the human being as such, whatever the outcome. And this is the kind of care that we in turn now owe or will owe. Of the brain-damaged, of those almost incapable of movement, of the autistic, of all such we have to say: this could have been us. Their mischances could

capable of full humanity?

have been ours, our good fortune could have been theirs. (It is this fact about us that makes our relationship to seriously disabled human beings quite other than our relationship to seriously disabled animals of other species; for a different, but not incompatible view see Jeff McMahan, 'Cognitive Disability, Misfortune and Justice', *Philosophy and Public Affairs* 25, 1, Winter 1996.)

There is then a complex relationship between the care and education that we have received and the care and education that we owe. But it is nonetheless in virtue of what we have received that we owe. So what then of those who have not received? Some of them may as a result have been quite unnecessarily disabled. Others who have succeeded in becoming independent practical reasoners look back to upbringings for which they have no reason to be grateful, upbringings which afford few good reasons or no good reason for acknowledging indebtedness. They may have been victims of sexual or other abuse as children, they may have been grossly deprived of elementary necessities, they may have been treated with systematic injustice, and have had few, if any, opportunities to learn which they did not make for themselves. If, in spite of this, they have nonetheless, through their own struggles against the obstacles that confronted them, emerged as independent practical reasoners, any debts that they may have may be far outweighed by the wrongs done to them. But notice that in saying this we are characterizing their condition in terms of just those norms of giving and receiving that are embodied in the relationships by which characteristically and generally independent practical reasoners are formed and sustained. It is only by reference to those norms that we are able to recognize the justice of their claim that, unlike others of us, they are not indebted. And the only appropriate response to their claims is first to acknowledge their justice, and secondly to recognize that the nature and effects of the wrongs done to those who utter them may be such that they now are among those to whom the rest of us are urgently called upon to give.

There are two distinct sources of such wrongs. One is

individual moral failure, arising from the vices of someone's character. The other is found in the systematic flaws of some particular set of social relationships in which the relationships of giving and receiving are embedded. These two sources are not unrelated. Defective systems of social relationships are apt to produce defective character. But even the best sets of social relationships cannot ensure that no one develops badly. And even the best sets of social relationship are to some important degree flawed. It could scarcely be otherwise.

Foucault was only the latest in a long line of thinkers — Augustine, Hobbes, and Marx are his most notable predecessors — to remind us that institutionalized networks of giving and receiving are also always structures of unequal distributions of power, structures well-designed both to mask and to protect those same distributions. So there are always possibilities and often actualities of victimization and exploitation bound up with participation in such networks. If we are not adequately aware of this, our practical judgments and reasoning will go badly astray. The virtues which we need in order to achieve both our own goods and the goods of others through participation in such networks only function as genuine virtues when their exercise is informed by an awareness of how power is distributed and of the corruptions to which its use is liable. Here as elsewhere in our lives we have to learn how to live both with and against the realities of power.

It is then the characteristic human condition to find ourselves occupying some position, and usually a series of positions over time, within some set of ongoing institutionalized relationships, relationships of family and household, of school or apprenticeship in some practice, of local community, and of the larger society, which present themselves under two aspects. Insofar as they are relationships of the kind of giving and receiving that I have described they are those relationships without which I and others could not become able to achieve and be sustained in achieving our goods. They are constitutive means to the end of our flourishing. But they will also generally be relationships that give expression to established hierarchies of power and of the uses of power, hierarchies and uses that, as instruments of domination and deprivation, often frustrate us in our movement towards our goods.

We generally find ourselves then in social situations that have this double-character, something that may be concealed from view when we speak too easily of "the" rules or "the" norms that govern and inform the structures of our social relationships. Sometimes there are two sets of rules coexisting, sometimes one and the same rule or rules may function now in one way, now in the other. Sometimes a way of life may be such that one set of rules is in active contention with the other and sometimes one set of rules may be subordinated to or even assimilated to the other. What these different and often changing relationships between these two kinds of rules reflect are the different outcomes of a range of small and large conflicts and struggles. The worst outcome is when the rules that enjoin giving and receiving have been substantially subordinated to or otherwise made to serve the purposes of power, the best when a distribution of power has been achieved which allows power to serve the ends to which the rules of giving and receiving are directed.

Consider the example of a family at any one of a number of stages of Western history, a family in which the parents have generally done well by their children, by the best standards available to them in their particular time and place. The mother has given them excellent prenatal and natal care, supported in this by the father, aunts, uncles, and grandparents, all of whom have contributed appropriately at each stage of the children's education. The father and mother not only generally put the children in the hands of good teachers, but were actively supportive of those teachers. The parents, that is, through exercising their authority prudently, showed themselves to be worthy of that authority. The children have thereby learned to recognize that prudent authority as an essential ingredient of what was given to them by way of care and education, so that they could become what they now are, independent practical reasoners. They have also understood in later adolescence or as young adults that they are in debt to their parents, other family members, and their teachers. And they also recognize that they in turn are bound to give, to their parents and other elders, when they are in need, to their own future children and indeed to all those whose needs become their responsibility. But now a source of conflict occurs.

The father, in order to be able to discharge his responsibilities to his wife and children, had had to abandon aspirations for a career as — no matter what, something that involved long and arduous training, but a later prospect of great riches, power, and glory. He now projects his phantasies concerning the career that he might have had on to one of his children. He allows his passionate wish that that child should become what he could not become to blind him to his child's need to become independent. And that child, already exercising her or his powers as an independent practical reasoner, has identified excellent reasons for not pursuing such a career. The father demands that she or he do so, invoking parental authority to legitimate threats of economic and other sanctions. The mother treats this refusal to obey the father as disgraceful. And there have been — indeed are — many cultures in which the established rules confer on the parents just the kind of authority that would justify this father and this mother in their attitudes.

If the child, however, were to do what her or his parents demand, she or he would fail in two closely related ways. She or he would show her or himself to be defective in the virtues of independent practical reasoning. And she or he would make a serious mistake about what they in fact owe to others, the kind of giving which according to the rules of giving and receiving is the counterpart to what she or he has received. So in this type of case the socially and culturally established rules defining parental authority are at odds with the rules of giving and receiving and the conception of parental authority which they legitimate.

The conflict between these two sets of rules is recurrent in Western cultures, and history and literature present us with many examples of the Bad Father, the Bad Mother, and such corresponding figures as the Bad King, the Bad Queen, and the

Bad Pope. Badness of course takes different social and cultural forms at different periods. The Bad Parent of the Victorian Age—Lytton Strachey's mother, for example, who imposed an education on him designed to make him into what he could never have become—was not at all the same as the Bad Parent of the Thirteenth Century—Thomas Aquinas's mother, who locked him up for a year with the purpose of making him abandon his Dominican vocation—but the underlying conflict between the two sets of rules with their two sets of requirements is the same. And in every period families can be placed along a spectrum with at one end familial patterns that express enforced conformity to the established distribution of power, and the other familial patterns that express those relationships of giving and receiving that are required for human flourishing.

What makes the bad parent bad is twofold. In demanding that the child give what the child does not owe the bad parent is unjust. And in presenting his or her claim as just, the bad parent is generally self-deceived or, if not self-deceived, is engaged in trying to deceive others. To justify these judgments we need to be able to justify the norms by appeal to which the bad parent is condemned, that is, the rules of giving and receiving more fully than I have hitherto done. So let me both reiterate and spell out a little further what I am claiming.

It is first of all and perhaps least controversially that the exercise of independent practical reasoning is one essential constituent to full human flourishing. It is not—as I have already insisted—that one cannot flourish at all, if unable to reason. Nonetheless not to be able to reason soundly at the level of practice is a grave disability. It is also a defect not to be independent in one's reasoning. By independence I mean both the ability and the willingness to evaluate the reasons for action advanced to one by others, so that one makes oneself accountable for one's endorsements of the practical conclusions of others as well as for one's own conclusions. One cannot then be an independent practical reasoner without being able to give to others an intelligible account of one's reasoning. But this account need not be in any substantial sense theoretical. In order to be sound practical reasoners farmers and flute-players do not need also to be logicians.

Practical deliberation, Aristotle remarked, is only about the means and not about the end (*Nicomachean Ethics* 1112b 33–34). It does not follow that we do not deliberate about particular ends, but only that, insofar as we do so, we treat those ends as means to still further ends. Aristotle's conception of actions that are a means to the achievement of some end includes both actions that effect the achievement of some end because of some contingent causal relationship between means and ends, as when shouting wakes someone up, and actions that are performed as constitutive parts of some whole, so that by their performance the whole is brought into being, as when making a particular move in a game of chess is a means to playing a game of chess, or as when following the rules of giving and receiving is constitutive of a way of life. The deliberative question which is to be answered in judgment and action by the practical reasoner—it need never have been made explicit—is of the form 'Given that such and such an end is to be achieved, what action is it best to perform as a means of achieving it?' If the initial response to this question is the further question 'But is this particular end the end that it is best for this particular individual or group to aim at here and now?' the reply to this second question will make or presuppose reference to some further end and be of the form 'Given that such and such a further end is to be achieved, this is/is not the immediate end to be aimed at by this particular individual or group here and now.' The reasoning which fully justifies practical judgment and action, on Aristotle's account (N. E. 1144a 31–34) refers us in the end to what is the first premise for all chains of sound practical reasoning, a premise of the form 'Since the good and the best is such and such . . . .' But of course in order to reason soundly about what it is best to do here and now, those who have the relevant virtues, and above all the virtue of prudent judgment, rarely need and may even be unable to make explicit the chain of justificatory reasoning that their immediate practical reasoning presupposes, while those who lack those virtues will be incapable of sound practical reasoning. What then makes it important for an account of the independent practical reasoner to make reference to this presupposed justificatory reasoning? The importance is of two kinds.

First, it makes plain how those who are to debate with each other rationally and fruitfully about means must already be in agreement about the relevant ends. It is not that there cannot be rational disagreement about ends, but if such disagreement is to be reasonable, if debate is not to be sterile, then there must be at some further and more fundamental level at least partial agreement about those ends to which the achievement of the ends under debate would or would not be a means. Why does this matter? Partly because, as I already emphasized, "On great matters we call upon others in deliberation, because we do not trust ourselves in deciding between alternatives" (N. E. 1112b 10–11). But it is also important that in our practical reasoning we often have to answer not only the question 'What is it best for me to do?' but also the question 'What is it best for us to do?' And we are commonly able to pose, let alone to answer, this latter question only because of the extent of our underlying agreements about goods and about the good.

Practical reasoning is by its nature, on the generally Aristotelian view that I have been taking, reasoning together with others, generally within some determinate set of social relationships. Those relationships are initially formed and then developed as the relationships through which each of us first achieves and is then supported in the status of an independent practical reasoner. They are generally and characteristically first of all relationships of the family and household, then of schools and apprenticeships, and then of the range of practices in which adults of that particular society and culture engage. The making and sustaining of those relationships is inseparable from the development of those dispositions and activities through which each is directed towards becoming an independent practical reasoner. So the good of each cannot be pursued without also pursuing the good of all those who participate in those relationships. For we cannot have a practically adequate understanding of our own good, of our own flourishing, apart from and independently of the flourishing of that whole set of social relationships in which we have found our place. Why not?

If I am to flourish to the full extent that is possible for a human being, then my whole life has to be of a certain kind, one in which I not only engage in and achieve some measure of success in the activities of an independent practical reasoner, but also receive and have a reasonable expectation of receiving the attentive care needed when I am very young, old and ill, or injured. So each of us achieves our good only if and insofar as others make our good their good by helping us through periods of disability to become ourselves the kind of human being— through acquisition and exercise of the virtues—who makes the good of others her or his good, and this not because we have calculated that, only if we help others, will they help us, in some trading of advantage for advantage. That would be the kind of human being who consults the good of others, only because and insofar as it is to her or his good to do so, a very different kind of human being, one deficient in the virtues, as I have characterized them.

For to participate in this network of relationships of giving and receiving as the virtues require, I have to understand that what I am called upon to give may be quite disproportionate to what I have received and that those to whom I am called upon to give may well be those from whom I shall receive nothing. And I also have to understand that the care that I give to others has to be in an important way unconditional, since the measure of what is required of me is determined in key part, even if not only, by their needs.

When a network of such familial, neighborhood, and craft relationships is in a flourishing state, when, that is, there is a flourishing local community, it will always be because those activities of the members of that community that aim at their common good are informed by their practical rationality. But those who benefit from that communal flourishing will include those least capable of independent practical reasoning, the very young and the very old, the sick, the injured, and the otherwise disabled, and their individual flourishing will be an important index of the flourishing of the whole community. For it is insofar as it is *need* that provides reasons for action for the members of some particular community that that community flourishes.

Note that on this account the good of the individual is not subordinated to the good of the community nor vice versa. The individual in order not just to pursue, but even to define her or his good in concrete terms has first to recognize the goods of the community as goods that she or he must make her own. The common good cannot therefore be understood as a summing of individual goods, as constructed out of them. At the same time although the pursuit of the common good of the community is, for all those capable of contributing to it, an essential ingredient of their individual good, the good of each particular individual is more than the common good. And there are of course common goods other than the goods of the overall community: the goods of families and of other groups, the goods of a variety of practices. Each individual as an independent practical reasoner has to answer the question of what place it is best that each of those goods should have in her or his life.

Just because the relevant form of community is constituted as a network of givers and receivers, both of whom need the virtues, the community's shared agreements must have as their subject matter not only goods, but also rules. For rule-following is an essential constituent of some of those virtues that both we ourselves and others must have, if we are to act adequately in those roles that we occupy within such a network. The types of action required by a particular virtue can never be specified exhaustively by any list of rules. But failure to observe certain rules may be sufficient to show that one is defective in some important virtues.

Consider, for example, the virtues of a trustworthy and reliable individual. If I am to be trustworthy and reliable, you must be able to trust me and to rely upon me, even when it is very much to my advantage to betray your confidence or very inconvenient for me to do what you are relying upon me to do.

I must be able to trust you and to rely on you, not only in the routine transactions of everyday life, important as these are, but also and especially when I am something of a burden and a nuisance, by reason of my disabilities. So I must know that you will be there, at times when you have promised to be there. I must know that you will not make promises that it would be unreasonable for you to make. I must know that in emergencies you will do what is needed and that you will not blench when some task for which you have taken responsibility turns out to be much more unpleasant—coping with vomiting or persistent bleeding or screaming, for example—or much more burdensome than expected.

I must also know that I can disclose confidential information to you without having to fear that you will then give it to someone else. And I must know that you do not engage in malicious gossip and that, no matter how absurd I may be, and no matter how witty you are, you will not make jokes that bring me into contempt. In all these cases what I have to know about you is that I can count on your regarding yourself as bound by certain rules, such rules as those that enjoin us to keep reasonable promises, to be punctual, to tell the truth, never to allow feelings of distaste or disgust to distract us from responsibilities for care, never to disclose confidential information and the like.

Yet there is more to being trustworthy and reliable than conformity to this or any set of rules. Part of being trustworthy and reliable is that we are able to recognize what trustworthiness and reliability require in situations where there is no rule to guide us. If it is right for me to convey certain information to you, then I will fail in trustworthiness, if I break the rule that prohibits lying. But when I have to answer the question whether I ought to disclose this particular piece of information about you to someone else, there will be situations in which no rule delivers an answer. Yet if I fail to make the right judgment, I shall have failed to show myself trustworthy, without having broken any rule. Or consider another example.

As a practical reasoner, I have to engage in conversation with others, conversation about what it would be best for me or them or us to do here and now, or next week, or next year. Here one relevant virtue is conversational justice. Conversational justice requires among other things, first that each of us speaks with candor, not pretending or deceiving or striking attitudes, and secondly that each takes up no more time than is justified by the importance of the point that she or he has to make and the arguments necessary for making it. The first of these requires conformity to certain rules, but the second requires what cannot be reduced to rules. As with other virtues, rule-following is part of, but does not exhaust what is required.

Without such virtues and the rule-following integral to their exercise, we will not only be deficient in discharging our responsibilities, but we will also be unable to deliberate adequately with others about the allocation of responsibilities. And, since such deliberation is necessary for achieving our common good, we will frustrate the achievement of that common good. It was upon this aspect of these rules that Aquinas focused attention, when he characterized them as included among the precepts of the natural law. On Aquinas's account, for a precept to be a law of any kind, it must be a precept of reason (*Summa Theologiae* 90, 1) directed to a common good (90, 2) and promulgated to a community by someone with the requisite authority (90, 3, 4). The precepts of the natural law are those precepts promulgated by God through reason without conformity to which human beings cannot achieve their common good.

The precepts of the natural law however include much more than rules. For among the precepts of the natural law are precepts which enjoin us to do whatever the virtues require of us (94, 3). We are enjoined to do whatever it is that courage or justice or temperateness demand on this or that occasion and always, in so acting, to act prudently. Notice that at the level of practice we need no reason for some particular action over and above that it is in this situation what one or more of the virtues requires. The acts required by the virtues are each of them worth performing for their own sake. They are indeed always also a means to something further, just because they are constitutive parts of human flourishing. But it is precisely as acts worth performing for their own sake that they are such parts.

To assert of a given action that it was performed for its own sake is not at all incompatible with saying of that same action that it was performed for the sake of that individual or these individuals to whose good it was directed. So acts of generosity, justice, and compassion are done for the sake of others and are worth doing in and for themselves. It is therefore always at the level of practice a sufficient answer to the question: 'Why did you do that?' to reply 'Because it was just', 'Because it was courageous', 'Because it was what a decent human being would do'. But at a more theoretical level we may and must respond to the question 'Why is this a sufficient answer?' And what makes it a sufficient answer is that it is only through the acquisition and exercise of the virtues that individuals and communities can flourish in a specifically human mode.

It is of course sometimes, even if rarely, the case that some reference to flourishing as the human *telos* has to be made explicit in reasoning at the level of practice. Normally and usually it is a concept whose application is tacitly presupposed, a concept that remains in the background. But there are in certain types of situation practically relevant reasons for bringing it into the foreground, for making explicit reference to it. One is when we fear that we may have made some error, because we have misconceived what, say, justice or courage or temperateness requires. It is in such situations that we may on occasion appeal to deductive argument in order to discover whether or not we have been mistaken. So we may argue that: Since human flourishing is such and such, that is, in Aristotle's terms, "Since the good and the best is such and such," then those qualities of mind and character that are virtues must be of such and such a kind, and since justice or courage or temperateness, as I have up till now conceived it, is not of this kind, I must have misconceived it and in consequence, misunderstood what virtue requires. Note that in this kind of retrospective reasoning, as in its prospective counterpart, the grasp of the concept of human flourishing to which the reasoner appeals had itself to be acquired in the course of practical experience. The stages through which we must go first in learning how to be independent practical reasoners, and then in extending our powers of reasoning to different and changing contexts, are also the stages through which we gradually acquire an adequate and reflective grasp of what human flourishing is, by learning to distinguish between those kinds of relationship that structure a flourishing individual and communal life from those kinds of relationship that inhibit or frustrate. And, since for a human being to flourish unqualifiedly *qua* human being, it is her or his life as a whole that must flourish, the individual has to learn through experience about the places both of independence and of dependence on others in the different stages of a flourishing life. It is insofar as an individual is able to articulate what she or he has thus learned that that individual is on occasion able to make explicit the first premise of her or his practical reasoning. So the practical learning needed, if one is to become a practical reasoner is the same learning needed, if one is to find one's place within a network of givers and receivers in which the achievement of one's individual good is understood to be inseparable from the achievement of the common good.

Yet this conception of the relationship of the common good to individual goods and of the place of both in practical reasoning is of course very much at odds with some widely influential conceptions of practical reasoning. Consider that according to which goodness is a matter of the satisfaction of desire: what is good, as I judge it, is what is good for me, what is good for me is to satisfy my preferences and what is best for me is to maximize my preference-satisfaction. So I begin by identifying my individual good and enquiring what means I should adopt, if I am to achieve it. I then discover that, if I do not cooperate with others in a way that takes account of their attempts to achieve their individual goods, the resulting conflicts will be such as to make it impossible for me to achieve my own good in anything but the shortest run and often enough not even then. So I and others find in a certain kind of cooperation a common good that is a means to and defined in terms of our individual goods.

On what terms is it rational for me to engage in such cooperation? They must be terms that allow each of the participants to regard this cooperation as rational for them and they must therefore include whatever set of constraints upon individual preference-maximization are necessary for each of the participants to understand such cooperation as rational for her or him. Each participant, that is, must have good reason to believe that maximization constrained by rules governing access to and engagement in cooperative bargaining with others will afford her or him more of what she or he wants than will unconstrained maximization.

Insofar as I am rational, I am bound to accept the constraints of those rules that ensure the kind of fair and secure bargaining through which each participant can best achieve the maximization of her or his preferences, but what other relationships I enter into is up to me. Perhaps as a matter of contingent fact I initially happen to find myself in certain familial or other social relationships. But such *de facto* involvement leaves entirely open the question of my commitments. I did not choose to be born to these particular parents or to have these aunts or teachers. What they gave me was up to them. What I do about it, if anything, is up to me. The concept of a debt has no application to any relationship or transaction that was not voluntarily undertaken. I am free both to calculate what is to my own best interest and to choose what my affective ties to others shall be.

My relationship to others will therefore, on this view, fall into two classes. There will be on the one hand those relationships designed for and justified by the advantages of the parties to the relationship. These will be bargaining relationships, governed by precepts derived from the theory of rational choice. There will be on the other hand those relationships that are the outcome of sympathy, of affective engagements that are voluntarily undertaken. And the difference is of crucial importance. As David Gauthier, who has provided the classic statement of this point of view for our generation, has written, "The demands of sympathy are quite distinct from those of rational choice, and only confusion results from treating them together" (*Morals by Agreement*, Oxford: Clarendon Press, 1986, p. 286).

The moral requirements imposed by rational choice extend only to those who are or may be our partners in cooperative bargaining. "Animals, the unborn, the congenitally handicapped and defective, fall beyond the pale of a morality tied to mutuality. The disposition to comply with moral constraints . . . may be rationally defended only within the scope of expected benefit" (p. 268). So everything to do with *our* relationships—*we* are of course neither handicapped nor defective—to nonhuman animals and to disabled human beings depends on the scope of *our* affective sympathies. Yet it is of course up to us what kinds and degrees of affection and sympathy we try to cultivate in ourselves and to encourage in our children and in others. That we have the particular affections and sympathies that we have at any given time is never a brute and unchangeable fact about us. But reason, as understood by the rational choice theorist, provides no direction for our sympathies.

This is of course not only a view taken by economic and philosophical theorists. It has provided more than one government with an ideological justification for its policies and many individuals with an ideological justification for their way of life, but it has been an ideology to which it has proved remarkably difficult to give wholly consistent adherence. And the inconsistencies that have been apparent are perhaps rooted in its inadequate dichotomizing account of social relationships: all social relationships are to be *either* relationships governed by bargaining undertaken for mutual advantage (market relationships provide the paradigm) *or* affective and sympathetic relationships. What is it that this dichotomy omits?

It is the extent to which in forms of social life that are viable for more than the shortest term each of these types of relationship is embedded in and needs to be characterized in terms of some set of relationships of giving and receiving of the kind that I have described. Consider first relationships of affection and sympathy and some of the complexities of those relationships. I have already noted that our affections and sympathies are generally, if not always, to a significant degree in our control, at least in the longer run. And this is important, because affection and sympathy are among those things that we owe to particular others. We always owe our children affection and children generally owe their parents responsive affection. We owe sympathy to others who are in pain or otherwise afflicted and we expect others to be likewise sympathetic in return. We owe our friends a different kind of affection from that which we owe to our children and we also owe them sympathetic understanding of their projects and predicaments. And the giving and receiving of affection and sympathy are of course not independent of, but closely related to those other types of giving and receiving that partially, but importantly constitute the relationships of parent and child, friend and friend, and the like.

Some individuals of course, perhaps by reason of their biochemistry, perhaps by reason of their upbringing, find it more difficult to have or to show the relevant kinds of feeling than do others. And some individuals by contrast have easily aroused feelings and tend to effusiveness and sentimentality in exhibiting them. What matters is not only that these are generally corrigible faults, but also that in judging them as faults we appeal to standards of appropriate feeling, of feeling that is proportionate to its objects, of feeling that is a mean between too little and too much. And the norms that govern feeling and determine its appropriateness or inappropriateness are inseparable from other norms of giving and receiving. For it is in giving and receiving in general that we exhibit affection and sympathy. The forms that the expression of these take do of course vary from culture to culture.

It is then only in the context of and by reference to norms of giving and receiving that we can spell out what is involved in different types of affective relationship. It is the acknowledgment of those norms that give us grounds for our expectations of others and for their expectations of us. Affective and sympathetic ties are always more than a matter of affection and sympathy. And in a similar way relationships of rational exchange, governed by norms to which it is to the advantage of each participant to adhere, are also embedded in and sustained by relationships governed by norms of uncalculated and unpredicted giving and receiving. So it is with those institutionalized relationships that make possible the exchanges of markets.

It is indeed true that "It is not from the benevolence of the butcher, the brewer or the baker, that we expect our dinner, but from their regard to their own interest" (Adam Smith, *The Wealth of Nations* I, ii). And just as butcher, brewer, and baker generally act with regard to their own interest, so too do their customers. But if, on entering the butcher's shop as an habitual customer I find him collapsing from a heart attack, and I merely remark 'Ah! Not in a position to sell me my meat to-day, I see,' and proceed immediately to his competitor's store to complete my purchase, I will have obviously and grossly damaged my *whole* relationship to him, including my economic relationship, although I will have done nothing contrary to the norms of the market. Less obviously and less grossly, even if I respond to his condition only by satisfying those minimum requirements that will enable me to rebut quasilegal accusations of irresponsibility—I call an ambulance and the moment the medical technicians arrive I leave—I will still have undermined my relationship to him and his, by my avoidance of my larger responsibility. Market relationships can only be sustained by being embedded in certain types of local nonmarket relationship, relationships of uncalculated giving and receiving, if they are to contribute to overall flourishing, rather than, as they so often in fact do, undermine and corrupt communal ties.

Norms of giving and receiving are then to some large degree presupposed both by our affective ties and by our market relationships. Detach them from this background presupposition in social practice and each becomes a source of vice: on the one hand a romantic and sentimental overvaluation of feeling as such, on the other a reduction of human activity to economic activity. These are complementary vices which can and sometimes do inform one and the same way of life. But to classify them as vices requires a larger justification than any that I have so far suggested. And such a justification requires a fuller account of the virtues of giving and receiving than I have so far provided.

10

The virtues of acknowledged dependence

Adam Smith's contrast between self-interested market behavior on the one hand and altruistic, benevolent behavior on the other, obscures from view just those types of activity in which the goods to be achieved are neither mine-rather-than-others' nor others'-rather-than-mine, but instead are goods that can only be mine insofar as they are also those of others, that are genuinely common goods, as the goods of networks of giving and receiving are. But if we need to act for the sake of such common goods, in order to achieve our flourishing as rational animals, then we also need to have transformed our initial desires in a way that enables us to recognize the inadequacy of any simple classification of desires as either egoistic or altruistic. The limitations and blindnesses of merely self-interested desire have been catalogued often enough. Those of a blandly genera- lized benevolence have received too little attention. What such benevolence presents us with is a generalized Other—one whose only relationship to us is to provide an occasion for the exercise of *our* benevolence, so that we can reassure ourselves about our own good will—in place of those particular others with whom we must learn to share common goods, and participate in ongoing relationships. What are the qualities needed for such participation?

To ask this question returns us to the discussion of the virtues and why they are needed. The emphasis in my earlier account was on the indispensable part that the virtues play in enabling us to move from dependence on the reasoning powers of others, principally our parents and teachers, to independence in our practical reasoning. And the virtues to which I principally referred were familiar items in Aristotelian and other catalogues: justice, temperateness, truthfulness, courage, and the like. But if we are to understand the virtues as enabling us to become independent practical reasoners, just because they also enable us to participate in relationships of giving and receiving through which our ends as practical reasoners are to be achieved, we need to extend our enquiries a good deal further, by recognizing that any adequate education into the virtues will be one that enables us to give their due to a set of virtues that are the necessary counterpart to the virtues of independence, the virtues of acknowledged dependence.

Conventional understandings of the virtues, even the conventional names for the virtues, may be unhelpful at this point. If, for example, we search for a name for the central virtue exhibited in relationships of receiving and giving, we will find that neither 'generosity' nor 'justice', as these have been commonly understood, will quite supply what is needed, since according to most understandings of the virtues one can be generous without being just and just without being generous, while the central virtue required to sustain this kind of receiving and giving has aspects both of generosity and justice. There is a Lakota expression 'wancantognaka' that comes much closer than any contemporary English expression. That Lakota word names the virtue of individuals who recognize responsibilities to immediate family, extended family, and tribe and who express that recognition by their participation in ceremonial acts of uncalculated giving, ceremonies of thanksgiving, of remembrance, and of the conferring of honor. 'Wancantognaka' names a generosity that I owe to all those others who also owe it to me (Lydia Whirlwind Soldier, 'Wancantognaka: the continuing Lakota custom of generosity', *Tribal College* Vii, 3, Winter 1995-6). Because I owe it, to fail to exhibit it is to fail in respect of justice; because what I owe is uncalculating giving, to fail to exhibit it is also to fail in respect of generosity. But it is not only among the Lakota that we find a recognition of this kind of relationship between justice and generosity.

Aquinas considers as one objection to the view that liberality is a part of the virtue of justice that justice is a matter of what is owed, and that therefore, when we give to another only what is owed to that other, we do not act with liberality. It is on this view the mark of the liberal, that is, the generous individual to give more than justice requires. To this Aquinas replies by distinguishing obligations that are a matter of strict justice, and of justice only, from the *decentia* required by liberality, actions that are indeed justly due to others, and are a minimum in the reckoning of what is due to others (*Summa Theologiae* IIa–IIae 117, 5). If we are to understand what Aquinas is saying here, we need to put it in context by considering also his treatment of the virtue of charity, or friendship towards God and human beings, of the virtue of taking pity, *misericordia*, and of the virtue of doing good, *beneficentia*. In discussing beneficence Aquinas emphasizes how in a single action these different virtues may be exemplified by different aspects of that action. Suppose that someone gives to another in significant need ungrudgingly, from a regard for the other as a human being in need, because it is the minimum owed to that other, and because in relieving the other's distress I relieve my distress at her or his distress. On Aquinas's account that individual at once acts liberally, from the beneficence of charity, justly, and out of taking pity. There is indeed that which is required by liberality, but not by justice, that which may be due from pity, but not from charity. But what the virtues require from us are characteristically types of action that are at once just, generous, beneficent, and done from pity. The education of dispositions to perform just this type of act is what is needed to sustain relationships of uncalculated giving and graceful receiving.

Such an education has to include, as we already noticed, the education of the affections, sympathies, and inclinations. The deprivations to which just generosity is the appropriate response are characteristically not only deprivations of physical care and intellectual instruction, but also and most of all deprivations of the attentive and affectionate regard of others. To act towards another as the virtue of just generosity requires is therefore to act from attentive and affectionate regard for that other. To this it is sometimes said that our affections are not ours to command. But, while in particular situations this may be true—I cannot here and now decide by an act of will to feel such and such—we can of course, as we also noticed earlier, cultivate and train our dispositions to feel, just as we can train our dispositions to act and indeed our dispositions to act with and from certain feelings. Just generosity then requires us to act from and with a certain kind of affectionate regard. When we are so required, not to act from inclination is always a sign of moral inadequacy, of a failure to act as our duty requires. Hume, unlike Kant, understood this very well. "Were not natural affection a duty, the care of children cou'd not be a duty: and 'twere impossible we cou'd have the duty in our eye in the attention we give to our offspring" (*A Treatise of Human Nature* III, ii, 1, ed. Selby-Bigge, p. 478). Do we then perhaps sometimes act from duty when we ought instead to act from inclination? Yes, replies Hume, we do so when we have recognized in ourselves the lack of some requisite motive: "a person who feels his heart devoid of that motive, may hate himself upon that account, and may perform the action without the motive, from a certain sense of duty, in order to acquire by practice that virtuous principle, or at least, to disguise to himself, as much as possible, his want of it" (p. 479).

I have already remarked that the practices of receiving and giving informed by particular just generosity are primarily exercised towards other members of our own community related to us by their and our roles. Yet this may have been misleading in more than one way. First of all we are often members of more than one community and we may find a place within more than one network of giving and receiving. Moreover we move in and out of communities. If therefore from now on I continue for simplicity's sake to speak of *the* community or network to which someone belongs, the reader should supply the missing arm of the disjunctions: 'community or communities', 'network or networks'. Secondly, it is important to the functioning of communities that among the roles 'that play a part in their shared lives there should be that of 'the stranger', someone from outside the community who has happened to arrive amongst us and to whom we owe hospitality, just because she or he is a stranger. Hospitality too is a duty that involves the inclinations, since it should be willing and ungrudging. But thirdly the scope of just generosity extends beyond the boundaries of community. Consider two testimonies from very different cultures, one from Sophocles, one from Mencius.

When, according to Sophocles, a shepherd was given the task of killing the infant Oedipus, he was instead moved by pity to dangerous disobedience and secretly entrusted the child to another shepherd, so that a home might be found for the child. And when Neoptolemus saw the open suppurating wound of Philoctetes and heard his screams of pain, he too was moved by pity to act otherwise than he had promised to act. Mencius said that "all human beings have the mind that cannot bear to see the sufferings of others . . . when human beings see a child fall into a well, they all have a feeling of harm and distress" and this not because they think that acting upon this feeling will gain them credit with others (and not because the child is a member of their household or community). What they will lack, if they do not respond to the child's urgent and dire need, just because it is urgent and dire need, is humanity, something without which we will be defective in our social relationships (see *The Book of Mencius* 2A:5, in Wing-tsit Chan, *A Sourcebook in Chinese Philosophy*, Princeton: Princeton University Press, 1963, p. 65). Such action-changing onsets of pity may of course sometimes be no more than momentary episodes in which a surge of nonrational feeling prompts a particular individual to act without further reflection. But Aquinas asserts that insofar as the occurrence of *misericordia* (I use the Latin rather than the English in order to avoid the association in English of 'pity' with condescension) is informed by the appropriate rational judgment, '*misericordia*' names a virtue and not just a passion (S. T. IIa–IIae, 30, 3), and that is to say that a capacity for *misericordia* that extends beyond communal obligations is itself crucial for communal life. Why is this so? *Misericordia* has regard to urgent and extreme need without respect of persons. It is the kind and scale of the need that dictates what has to be done, not whose need it is. And what each of us needs to know in our communal relationships is that the attention given to *our* urgent and extreme needs, the needs characteristic of disablement, will be proportional to the need and not to the relationship. But we can rely on this only from those for whom *misericordia* is one of the virtues. So communal life itself needs this virtue that goes beyond the boundaries of communal life. And it is the virtue and not just the capacity for sentiment that is needed. Sentiment, unguided by reason, becomes sentimentality and sentimentality is a sign of moral failure. What then is the virtue? If I turn immediately to Aquinas's account, it is in part because, although the practical recognition of this virtue is often widespread, theoretical accounts are rare and I know of no other similarly extended account. What then does Aquinas say?

He treats *misericordia* as one of the effects of charity, and, since charity is a theological virtue, and the theological virtues are due to divine grace, an incautious reader might suppose that Aquinas does not recognize it as a secular virtue. But this would be a mistake. Charity in the form of *misericordia* is recognizably at work in the secular world and the authorities whom Aquinas cites on its nature, and whose disagreements he aspires to resolve, include Sallust and Cicero as well as Augustine. *Misericordia* then has its place in the catalogue of the virtues, independently of its theological grounding. Towards whom is it directed?

To those, whoever they are, who are afflicted by some considerable evil, especially when it is not the immediate outcome of the afflicted individual's choices (IIa–IIae, 30, 1), a qualification that perhaps itself needs qualifying. Extreme and urgent necessity on the part of another in itself provides a stronger reason for action than even claims based upon the closest of familial ties (31, 3). And when such need is less extreme and urgent, it still may on occasion be rightly judged to outweigh the claims of familial or other immediate social ties. (This is a feature of Aquinas's account that goes unnoticed in Arnhart's otherwise illuminating argument, designed to show how Aquinas's theses about the natural law are compatible with a biological understanding of human nature, op. cit., p. 260.) There is no rule to decide such cases and the virtue of prudence has to be exercised in judgment (31, 3, ad. 1). It might then seem that we have two distinct and sometimes competing kinds of claim that might be made upon us: on the one hand by those who stand to us in some determinate social relationship by virtue of their place in the same community as ourselves, and on the other by those severely afflicted in some way, whether or not they stand in such a relationship to us. Aquinas's account of the virtue of *misericordia* however requires us to reject this contrast, at least as I have so far formulated it.

Misericordia is grief or sorrow over someone else's distress, says Aquinas, just insofar as one understands the other's distress as one's own. One may do this because of some preexisting tie to the other—the other is already one's friend or kin—or because in understanding the other's distress one recognizes that it could instead have been one's own. But what is involved in such an understanding? *Misericordia* is that aspect of charity whereby we supply what is needed by our neighbor and among the virtues that relate us to our neighbor *misericordia* is the greatest (30, 4). So to understand another's distress as our own is to recognize that other as neighbor, and, says Aquinas, in all matters with regard to love of the neighbor, "it does not matter whether we say 'neighbor' as in *I John 4*, or 'brother' as in *Leviticus 19*, or 'friend', since all these refer to the same affinity." But to recognize another as brother or friend is to recognize one's relationship to them as being of the same kind as one's relationship to other members of one's own community. So to direct the virtue of *misericordia* towards others is to extend one's communal relationships so as to include those others within those relationships. And we are required from now on to care about them and to be concerned about their good just as we care about others already within our community.

I have so far catalogued three salient characteristics of relationships that are informed by the virtue of just generosity: they are communal relationships that engage our affections, they extend beyond the long-term relationships of the members of a community to each other to relationships of hospitality to passing strangers, and, through the exercise of the virtue of *misericordia*, they include those whose urgent need confronts the members of such a community. And in speaking of the type of action that issues from just generosity, I have used the word 'uncalculating', but this predicate now has to be qualified. Just generosity requires us to be uncalculating in this sense, that we can rely on no strict proportionality of giving and receiving. As I have said before, those from whom I hope to and perhaps do receive are very often, even if not always, not the same people as those to whom I gave. And what I am called upon to give has no predetermined limits and may greatly exceed what I have received. I may not calculate what I owe on the basis of what others have given me. There is however another sense in which prudent calculation is not only permitted, but required by just generosity. If I do not work, so as to acquire property, I will have nothing to give. If I do not save, but only consume, then, when the time comes when my help is urgently needed by my neighbor, I may not have the resources to provide that help. If I give to those not really in urgent need, then I may not have enough to give to those who are. So industriousness in getting, thrift in saving, and discrimination in giving are required. And these are further aspects of the virtue of temperateness.

Notice that to these virtues of giving must be added virtues of receiving: such virtues as those of knowing how to exhibit gratitude, without allowing that gratitude to be a burden, courtesy towards the graceless giver, and forbearance towards the inadequate giver. The exercise of these latter virtues always involves a truthful acknowledgment of dependence. And they are therefore virtues bound to be lacking in those whose forgetfulness of their dependence is expressed in an unwillingness to remember benefits conferred by others. One outstanding example, even perhaps *the* outstanding example of this type of bad character and also of a failure to recognize its badness is Aristotle's *megalopsychos*, about whom Aristotle remarks approvingly, that he "is ashamed to receive benefits, because it is a mark of a superior to confer benefits, of an inferior to receive them" (*Nicomachean Ethics* 1124b 9–10). So the *megalopsychos* is forgetful of what he has received, but remembers what he has given, and is not pleased to be reminded of the former, but hears the latter recalled with pleasure (12–18). We recognize here an illusion of self-sufficiency, an illusion apparently shared by Aristotle, that is all too characteristic of the rich and powerful in many times and places, an illusion that plays its part in excluding them from certain types of communal relationship. For like virtues of giving, those of receiving are needed in order to sustain just those types of communal relationship through which the exercise of these virtues first has to be learned. It is perhaps unsurprising then that from the standpoint of such relationships urgent need and necessity have to be understood in a particular light. What someone in dire need is likely to need immediately here and now is food, drink, clothing and shelter. But, when these first needs have been met, what those in need then most need is to be admitted or readmitted to some recognized position within some network of communal relationships in which they are acknowledged as a participating member of a deliberative community, a position that affords them both empowering respect from others and self-respect. Yet such respect for others is not the fundamental form of human regard that is required for this kind of communal life. Why not?

Those in dire need both within and outside a community generally include individuals whose extreme disablement is such that they can never be more than passive members of the community, not recognizing, not speaking or not speaking intelligibly, suffering, but not acting. I suggested earlier that for the rest of us an important thought about such individuals is 'I might have been that individual.' But that thought has to be translated into a particular kind of regard. The care that we ourselves need from others and the care that they need from us require a commitment and a regard that is not conditional upon the contingencies of injury, disease and other afflictions. My regard for another is always open to being destroyed by what the other does, by serious lies, by cruelty, by treachery, by victimization, by exploitation, but if it is diminished or abolished by what happens to the other, by her or his afflictions, then it is not the kind of regard necessary for those communal relationships—including relationships to those outside the community—through which our common good can be achieved.

11

The political and social structures of the common good

What are the types of political and social society that can embody those relationships of giving and receiving through which our individual and common goods can be achieved? They will have to satisfy three conditions. First they must afford expression to the political decision-making of independent reasoners on all those matters on which it is important that the members of a particular community be able to come through shared rational deliberation to a common mind. So there will have to be institutionalized forms of deliberation to which all those members of the community who have proposals, objections and arguments to contribute have access. And the procedures of decision-making will have to be generally acceptable, so that both deliberation and decisions are recognizable as the work of the whole.

Secondly, in a community in which just generosity is counted among the central virtues the established norms of justice will have to be consistent with the exercise of this virtue. No single simple formulation will be capable of capturing the different kinds of norm that will be necessary for different kinds of just relationship. Between independent practical reasoners the norms will have to satisfy Marx's formula for justice in a socialist society, according to which what each receives is proportionate to what each contributes. Between those capable of giving and those who are most dependent and in most need of receiving—children, the old, the disabled—the norms will have to satisfy a revised version of Marx's formula for justice in a communist society, "From each according to her or his ability, to each, so far as is possible, according to her or his needs' (*Critique of the Gotha Program*, I). Marx of course understood his second formula as having application only in an as yet unrealizable future. And we must recognize that limited economic resources allow only for its application in imperfect ways. But without its application, even if imperfectly, even if *very* imperfectly, we will be unable to sustain a way of life characterized both by effective appeals to desert and by effective appeals to need, and so by justice to and for both the independent and the dependent.

Thirdly, the political structures must make it possible both for those capable of independent practical reason and for those whose exercise of reasoning is limited or nonexistent to have a voice in communal deliberation about what these norms of justice require. And the only way in which the latter can have a voice is if there are others who are able and prepared to stand proxy for them and if the role of proxy is given a formal place in the political structures.

What I am trying to envisage then is a form of political society in which it is taken for granted that disability and dependence on others are something that all of us experience at certain times in our lives and this to unpredictable degrees, and that consequently our interest in how the needs of the disabled are adequately voiced and met is not a special interest, the interest of one particular group rather than of others, but rather the interest of the whole political society, an interest that is integral to their conception of their common good. What kind of society might possess the structures necessary to achieve a common good thus conceived?

If at this point we turn for assistance to recent social and political philosophy, we will be for the most part disappointed, since with rare exceptions work in that area ignores questions about the common goods of associations and relationships that are intermediate between on the one hand the nation-state and on the other the individual and the nuclear family. Yet it is with just this intermediate area that we shall need to be concerned, since those whose relationships embody both a recognition of the independence of practical reasoners and an acknowledgment of the facts of human dependence, and for whom therefore the virtue of just generosity is a key virtue, presuppose in their activities, explicitly, or more usually implicitly, the sharing of a common good that is constitutive of a type of association that can be realized neither in the forms of the modern state nor in those of the contemporary family.

Why not? What is it about the modern state and the contemporary family that renders them incapable of providing the kind of communal association within which this type of common good can be achieved? Let me consider each in turn. Modern nation-states are governed through a series of compromises between a range of more or less conflicting economic and social interests. What weight is given to different interests varies with the political and economic bargaining power of each and with its ability to ensure that the voices of its protagonists are heard at the relevant bargaining tables. What determines both bargaining power and such ability is in key part money, money used to provide the resources to sustain political power: electoral resources, media resources, relationships to corporations. This use of money procures very different degrees and kinds of political influence for different interests. And the outcome is that although most citizens share, although to greatly varying extents, in such public goods as those of a minimally secure order, the distribution of goods by government in no way reflects a common mind arrived at through widespread shared deliberation governed by norms of rational enquiry. Indeed the size of modern states would itself preclude this. It does not follow that relationships to the nation-state, or rather to the various agencies of government that collectively compose it, are unimportant to those who practice the politics of the virtues of acknowledged dependence. No one can avoid having some significant interest in her or his relationships to the nation-state just because of its massive resources, its coercive legal powers, and the threats that its blundering and distorted benevolence presents. But any rational relationship of the governed to the government of modern states requires individuals and groups to weigh any benefits to be derived from it against the costs of entanglement with it, at least so far as that aspect of states is concerned in which they are and present themselves as giant utility companies.

There is of course another aspect of the modern state in which it presents itself as the guardian of our values and from time to time invites us to die for it. This invitation is one issued by every ruling power that asserts its legitimate and justifiable political and legal sovereignty over its subjects. For no state can justify that assertion unless it is able to provide at least minimal security for its subjects from external aggression and from internal criminality. And the provision of such security generally requires that there be police officers, firefighters, and soldiers prepared, if need arise—and it does arise remarkably often—to give up their lives in the course of their duties. But the importance of the good of public security, although it is a good served by this admirable devotion, and although it is a good without which none of us in our various local communities could achieve our common goods, must not be allowed to obscure the fact that the shared public goods of the modern nation-state are not the common goods of a genuine nation-wide community and, when the nation-state masquerades as the guardian of such a common good, the outcome is bound to be either ludicrous or disastrous or both. For the counterpart to the nation-state thus misconceived as itself a community is a misconception of its citizens as constituting a *Volk*, a type of collectivity whose bonds are simultaneously to extend to the entire body of citizens and yet to be as binding as the ties of kinship and locality. In a modern, large scale nation-state no such collectivity is possible and the pretense that it is is always an ideological disguise for sinister realities. I conclude then that insofar as the nation-state provides necessary and important public goods, these must not be confused with the type of common good for which communal recognition is required by the virtues of acknowledged dependence, and that insofar as the rhetoric of the nation-state presents it as the provider of something that is indeed, in this stronger sense, a common good, that rhetoric is a purveyor of dangerous fictions.

The virtues of acknowledged dependence and the virtues of independence require for their practice a very different kind of shared pursuit of a common good. Where the virtues of acknowledged dependence are practiced, there will have to be a common mind as to how responsibilities for and to dependent others are allocated and what standards of success or failure in discharging these responsibilities are appropriate. And, where the virtues of independent practical reasoning are practiced, such a common mind will have to emerge from shared deliberation, so that social agreement on responsibilities will not only be, but be seen to be rationally justified. Hence those who practice both sets of virtues will have a double attitude to the nation-state. They will recognize that it is an ineliminable feature of the contemporary landscape and they will not despise the resources that it affords. It may and on occasion does provide the only means for removing obstacles to humane goals and we all have reason, for example, to be very grateful indeed to those who secured the passage of the Americans with Disabilities Act and to those who have used its provisions constructively and creatively. But they will also recognize that the modern state cannot provide a political framework informed by the just generosity necessary to achieve the common goods of networks of giving and receiving.

If then the nation-state cannot provide a form of association directed towards the relevant type of common good, what of the family? Families at their best are forms of association in which children are first nurtured, and then educated for and initiated into the activities of an adult world in which their parents' participatory activities provide them both with resources and models. It follows that the quality of life of a family is in key part a function of the quality of the relationships of the individual members of the family to and in a variety of other institutions and associations: workplaces, schools, parishes, sports clubs, trade union branches, adult education classes, and the like. And it is insofar as children learn to recognize and to pursue as their own, and parents and other adult members of the family continue to recognize and to pursue, the goods internal to the practices of which such associations and institutions are the milieu that the goods of family life are realized. The family flourishes only if its social environment also flourishes. And since the social environments of families vary a great deal, so do the modes of flourishing of families. All happy families are not alike and only a very great novelist could have got away with telling us otherwise. And as it is with the strengths and achievements of family life, so it is also with its weaknesses and failures. They too are inseparable from features of the social environment of the family. (I do not want to suggest by this that families cannot sometimes flourish in highly unfavorable conditions. They can and do. But, when they can and do, it is always because the family members and more especially the parents have been able to construct for that family a range of activities and opportunities that substitute for those of a more favorable social environment. So, for example, for a family living successfully in conditions of extreme isolation, perhaps a hundred miles from their nearest neighbors, the activity of workplace, of school, of parish, and of play may all become activities of the household. That household will have become a microcosm of community and not only a family. Yet this must clearly be an exceptional type of case.)

Generally and characteristically then the goods of family life are achieved in and with the goods of various types of local community. And generally and characteristically the common good of a family can only be achieved in the course of achieving the common goods of the local community of which it is a part. It is because of the family's lack of self-sufficiency that the type of common good recognition of which is required by the virtues of acknowledged dependence cannot be achieved within the family, at least insofar as the family is conceived of as a distinct and separate social unit. Yet families are of course key and indispensable constituents of local community and there are many areas of family life in which the exercise of the virtues of acknowledged dependence is called for. Indeed, as I suggested earlier, the relationships of parents to young children and of adults to their elderly parents are both paradigm cases of relationships that can be sustained only by those virtues. And so is the relationship of the able and independent members of a family to other members who are temporarily or permanently disabled and largely or wholly dependent.

Neither the state nor the family then is the form of association whose common good is to be both served and sustained by the virtues of acknowledged dependence. It must instead be some form of local community within which the activities of families, workplaces, schools, clinics, clubs dedicated to debate and clubs dedicated to games and sports, and religious congregations may all find a place. What kind of place then are those who are temporarily or permanently disabled able to have in such a community? What kind of recognition is the recognition required to sustain respect both for them and for those not disabled, as well as their self-respect? It will build upon that regard for each individual, however badly disabled, that I characterized earlier. But it will add to that regard a recognition that each member of the community is someone from whom we may learn and may have to learn about our common good and our own good, and who always may have lessons to teach us about those goods that we will not be able to learn elsewhere. It is not primarily because others find what we achieve worthwhile that we are owed this respect. For even at those times when we are disabled so that we cannot engage in worthwhile projects we are still owed by others and we still owe to others that attentive care without which neither we nor they can learn what we have to teach each other.

When I speak of learning what our common good is, I am, as previously, referring to how we acquire practical knowledge of that good, not the mastery of some set of theoretical formulas, but the acquisition of a directedness towards that

good embodied in our everyday practice. I have already emphasized that we learn what our common good is, and indeed what
our own individual goods are, not primarily and never only by
theoretical reflection, but in everyday shared activities and the
evaluations of alternatives that those activities impose. And I
have also emphasized that we can fail to learn what we need to
learn and this by reason of a number of types of failure, of
which I listed three: inability to separate ourselves from and to
stand in judgment upon our desires, lack of adequate self-
knowledge, and failure to recognize the nature of our dependence on others. Let me consider one example of what can be
learned and sometimes only learned from relationships with the
disabled which may involve the discovery in ourselves of any of
these three sources of error with a resulting set of false and
misleading practical judgments.

Consider that kind of disablement which consists in gross
disfigurement of the surface of body parts, perhaps of a swollen,
inflamed, scarred, and secretion-exuding face, where the horrifying and disgusting appearance of the sufferer becomes an
obstacle to addressing her or him as a human being. Nurses or
physicians whose duty it is to understand the sufferer's appearance as a set of symptoms of an underlying condition have
perhaps an easier task than the rest of us who need to find some
way of avoiding both the mistakes involved in pretending that
the sufferer does not in fact present an horrifying appearance
and those involved in being too distracted by that appearance to
be able to deal rationally with the sufferer. What we may learn
about ourselves from grappling with these difficulties is in part
the nature and degree of the value that we have hitherto placed
upon a pleasing appearance in other human beings and indeed
in ourselves and the errors in those judgments of value.

Social psychological studies confirm what common observa-
tion suggests that many of us are too often influenced by facial
and other appearance in a variety of contexts (see, for example,
K. Dion, D. Berscheid, and E. Walster 'What Is Beautiful Is
Good', *Journal of Personality and Social Psychology* 24, 1972;
S. E. Asch reported in 'Forming Expressions of Personality',

Journal of Social Psychology 41, 1946, that 77% of his subjects inferred from a description of someone as intelligent, skillful, industrious, warm, determined, practical, and cautious that that individual would also be good-looking. *The Times* of London reported on May 26, 1998, an NOP poll finding in Britain that one person in three believes that those in wheelchairs are less intelligent). And more generally it is too often the case that the weight that we give to a particular consideration in a piece of uttered reasoning is partly determined by who uttered it in what kind of voice and with what kind of facial expression. We therefore need to learn how to dissociate the evaluation of personal qualities and of reasoning from physical appearance and from manner of presentation. In so doing we may discover what we had not hitherto suspected: that we have not up till now been able to separate ourselves from feelings of dislike, disgust and even horror in responding to the facial appearances of certain types of other and so we have not been able to exercise critical judgment in respect of those feelings; that we have been lacking in adequate self-knowledge in failing to understand the full range of judgments that are influenced irrelevantly by such feelings; and that, in responding to those whose appearance has affronted us, we have assumed that from *them* at least we could have nothing to learn. We discover, that is, in our encounters with the disabled hitherto unrecognized sources of error in our own practical reasoning. And, insofar as these derived from the hitherto dominant norms of our social environment, we will have to transform that environment as well as ourselves, if we are to be freed from such errors in our shared deliberative reasoning.

If we are unable to free ourselves from these sources of error, we will continue to obscure what it is in both ourselves and others to which we ought to be responding in different contexts and we ourselves will continue to lead distorted lives. Note that this does not mean that we ought not to distinguish what is pleasing in appearance from what is unpleasing and both from what is horrifying, or that we should not continue to recognize that a handsome appearance and an engaging manner are good things to possess. But we will be mistaken as to the nature and limits of their goodness, if we allow ourselves to be seduced by their attractiveness into undervaluing those qualities and arguments that have to make themselves known through disfigurement and disablement.

What blinds us to our own defects in self-knowledge may also blind us as to qualities of others. So those captivated by appearance and presentation may not be able to identify, let alone understand, examples of the courage and gracefulness of spirit that can be hard-won responses to afflictions of disfigurement and disablement, and this will be a failure to understand the importance of some virtues of acknowledged dependence. Insofar as we do not identify and understand these virtues, it becomes the more likely that we ourselves will not know how to practice them, if and when we in turn undergo either disfiguring disablement, or one of those many other forms of disablement—including those of normal aging—that need the resources provided by those same virtues.

To this it may be said that so far I may have argued a relatively uncontroversial case, but one that could not be made out in respect of more extreme forms of disability and dependence, such as those in which the physically and mentally incapacitated are incapable of all or all but the most minimal responses to others, human beings who do not or no longer achieve the status of Lockean persons, human beings whose potentialities for rationality or affective response have been permanently frustrated. It will be urged that of such we can only say that at most they can be passive objects of benevolence designed to limit their suffering, beings whose existence can only be a cost, but not in any way a benefit to others. How could *they* be our teachers? This is a powerful and widely influential view. Its presupposition is that caring for and giving to those others who can make no voluntary return to me can only be costs and burdens. Towards them I may adopt an attitude of benevolence, but my relationship to them must be one-sided. But this is a mistake. What they give us is the possibility of learning something essential, what it is for someone else to be wholly entrusted to our care, so that we are answerable for their well-being. Everyone of us has, as an infant, been wholly entrusted to someone else's care, so that they were answerable for our well-being. Now we have the opportunity to learn just what it is that we owe to such individuals by learning for ourselves what it is to be so entrusted. There are two aspects of any such relationship. One involves the actual giving of life-sustaining and pain-abating physical and sometimes psychological care, the whole messy and immensely fatiguing business of bedpans and vomit and changing sheets, of dealing with sores or tantrums or wandering incoherence, of giving medicines and bandaging wounds. The other is a matter of the role of the proxy for those disabled who are unable to speak for themselves. The proxy's role is to speak for those thus disabled both inside and outside the community in just the way that that particular disabled individual would have done so for her or himself, had she or he still been able to speak. The radically disabled individual needs someone who will speak for her or him as, so to speak, a second self. And, since we are all potentially liable to this extreme condition, we all of us now or later may need someone to be our second self, to speak for us. Yet no one will be able to speak adequately for me who does not already know me. Such an individual will generally need to know how I have judged my good in various situations in the past and what the reasoning was by which I supported my judgments. For, only if they know this, will they be able to speak for *me*, as I would have done for myself. This relationship then between those who have become radically disabled, so that others have to speak for them, generally has to be rooted in previously existing relationships of friendship.

Notice that this relationship between particular radically disabled individuals, unable to speak for themselves, and those who are able to speak for them is therefore in some respects very different from the relationship between parents and infants. There may be and sometimes is the same degree of dependence and there may be and sometimes is the same obligation to identify and attempt to achieve the good of those entrusted to one's care. But it would be mere confusion for the parent of an infant to ask what judgment about its good the child would make in this or that situation, since what judgments about its good the child will make will depend in key part on how the parents bring up the child. The parents have first to make their own judgments about the good of the child. And sometimes of course, when someone finds entrusted to her or his care a disabled person in a long-lasting coma, about whose prior judgments they have no knowledge, there is no alternative but, as with the infant, to make one's own judgments about the good of the other. But in less extreme cases that is not at all the situation, and we should therefore make it our aim that, so far as possible, each individual contributes to the shared deliberations of the community in her or his own voice, as an independent political reasoner.

Political reasoning at the level of practice is not a special kind of reasoning, one distinct from ordinary practical reasoning. One cannot generally become an effective practical reasoner without becoming in some measure a political reasoner, and this for two reasons. First, because participants in networks of giving and receiving are only able to identify their individual goods in the course of identifying their common goods, and because their identification of those common goods can only be achieved by contributing to and learning from shared deliberation with those others whose common goods they are, an ability to reason practically about the common good is indispensable. But to reason together about the common good is to reason politically.

Secondly, so many of our goods, individual as well as common, are shared goods that generally my decisions about what part certain goods are to play in my life will not be and cannot be independent of our decisions about what part those goods are to play in the life of our community. I will not be able to find a place, whether a larger or smaller place, for dramatic art in my own life—as amateur or professional actor, as director or stagehand, as a member of the orchestra or the audience—in a community in which the goods of theater are not given a certain priority in the allocation of communal resources. It is in and through political decisions about these priorities that we determine the range of possibilities open for the shaping of our individual lives and, if we exclude ourselves or are excluded by others from contributing to such political decision-making, we diminish the scope and effectiveness of our decision-making.

This suggests that the account advanced so far of the prerequisites for a political community whose common good would be that of social networks of giving and receiving badly needs to be supplemented, if it is not to be misleading. For I have asked what attitudes of regard we should take to each other, whether able or disabled, if we are to satisfy the require- ments of such virtues as that of just generosity, as though we could first answer that question and only then as a secondary matter enquire what kinds of political structures might give expression to such attitudes. But it now becomes clear that these attitudes of regard must be understood from the outset as political attitudes. To treat someone else as someone for whom we have a regard because of what, one way or another, they contribute to our shared education in becoming rational givers and receivers is to accord them political recognition. It is to treat them as someone whom it would be wrong to ignore or to exclude from political deliberation.

This conception of political reasoning as one aspect of everyday practical reasoning has as its counterpart a conception of political activity as one aspect of the everyday activity of every adult capable of engaging in it. The contrast is with the conception of political activity embodied in the modern state, according to which there is a small minority of the population who are to make politics their active occupation and preoccupa- tion, professional and semiprofessional politicians, and a huge largely passive majority who are to be mobilized only at periodic intervals, for elections or national crises. Between the political elites on the one hand and the larger population on the other there are important differences, as in, for example, how much or how little information is required and provided for each. A modern electorate can only function as it does, so long as it has only a highly simplified and impoverished account of the issues that are presented to it. And the modes of presentation through which elites address electorates are designed to conceal as much as to reveal.

These are not accidental features of the politics of modern states any more than is the part that money plays in affording influence upon the decision-making process. The sometimes revolutionary struggles of the past that broke down the barriers to achieving modern citizenship—to abolish slavery, to extend the suffrage, especially to women, to secure for the labor movement defenses against capitalist exploitation and victimization—involved degrees and kinds of effective political participation that are quite as alien to the democratic forms of the politics of the contemporary state as they are to nondemocratic forms. It is not at all, as I have already stressed, that the politics of the state have become unimportant. There are numerous crucial needs of local communities that can only be met by making use of state resources and invoking the interventions of state agencies. But it is the quality of the politics of local communities that will be crucial in defining those needs adequately and in seeing to it that they are met.

It is therefore a mistake, the communitarian mistake, to attempt to infuse the politics of the state with the values and modes of participation in local community. It is a further mistake to suppose that there is anything good about local community as such. The relatively small-scale character and the face-to-face encounters and conversations of local community are necessary for the shared achievement of the common goods of those who participate in the rational deliberation needed to sustain networks of giving and receiving, but, absent the virtues of just generosity and of shared deliberation, local communities are always open to corruption by narrowness, by complacency, by prejudice against outsiders and by a whole range of other deformities, including those that arise from a cult of local community.

This is one point at which the discussions of moral and political philosophers benefit from becoming historical and sociological. We need to set side by side for comparative study examples of different types of local community, examples of such communities at their best and at their worst, and most of all examples of communities that have been or are open to alternative possibilities and that sometimes move towards the better and sometimes towards the worse. So it would be instructive to look at the history of some fishing communities in New England over the past hundred and fifty years and to examine the different ways in which at different times their virtues have enabled them to cope with the stress of adversity and with the stress of prosperity. And it would be similarly instructive to examine the history of Welsh mining communities and of a way of life informed by the ethics of work at the coal face, by a passion for the goods of choral singing and of rugby football and by the virtues of trade union struggle against first coal-owners and then the state. Such examples can be multiplied: farming cooperatives in Donegal, Mayan towns in Guatemala and Mexico, some city-states from a more distant past.

What such comparative studies will bring home to us is both the variety of social forms within which networks of giving and receiving can be institutionalized and the variety of ways in which such networks can be sustained and strengthened or weakened and destroyed. Different conditions pose different threats that in turn require different responses. Yet the tasks that have to be undertaken to meet those threats share a great deal in common. So it is, for example, with the tasks of providing for the security of a local community from internal crime or external aggression, tasks that can never safely be handed over completely to the agencies of the state. (On occasion it is the danger presented by just those agencies that has to be guarded against.) Those who perform such tasks on behalf of the community are asked by the community to be prepared, if necessary, to risk their lives, but to ask this can only be justified, if those who accept this risk can be confident that they, if disabled, or their dependents, if they die, will receive adequate care. The defense of a community whose structures are governed by norms of relatively uncalculated giving and receiving, if it is in good order, will itself be similarly structured. Yet the forms taken by those structures will vary with the culture and the history of the community.

What extended comparative study of the varying characteristics of communities that embody networks of giving and receiving may teach us is how better to identify what relationships of the relevant kinds of giving and receiving already exist in our own local community and how perhaps to greater extent than we have realized there is already a degree of shared recognition of the common good. About such communities we will need to bear in mind three things. First, even when they are at their best, the exercise of shared deliberative rationality is always imperfect and what should impress us is not so much the mistakes made and the limitations upon its exercise at any particular stage as the ability through time and conflict to correct those mistakes and to move beyond those limitations. The exercise of practical relationships in communities always has a history and it is the direction of that history that is important.

Secondly, the politics of such communities, when they are at their best or are at least moving in the right direction, is not a politics of competing interests in the way in which the politics of the modern state is. For the basic political question is what resources each individual and group needs, if it is to make its particular contribution to the common good, and, insofar as the community if in good order, it is to the interest of all that each should be able to make its contribution. Of course because local communities are always to some degree imperfect, competing interests are always apt to emerge. And it is therefore important that, so far as is possible, communities are structured so as to limit such emergence. Economically what matters is that there should be relatively small inequalities of income or wealth. For gross inequality of income or wealth is by itself always liable to generate conflicts of interest and to obscure the possibility of understanding one's social relationships in terms of a common good.

This is of course only one example of how economic considerations will have to be subordinated to social and moral considerations, if a local community that is a network of giving and receiving is to survive, let alone thrive. There may have to be self-imposed limits to labor mobility for the sake of the continuities and the stabilities of families and other institutions. There will have to be what from an economic point of view is disproportionate investment in types of education of children that are not economically productive. Everyone, so far as is possible, will have to take their turn in performing the tedious and the dangerous jobs, in order to avoid another disruptive form of social inequality. These are of course Utopian standards, not too often realized outside Utopia, and only then, as I have already suggested, in flawed ways. But trying to live by Utopian standards is not Utopian, although it does involve a rejection of the economic goals of advanced capitalism. For the institutional forms through which such a way of life is realized, although economically various, have this in common: they do not promote economic growth and they require some significant degree of insulation from and protection from the forces generated by outside markets. Most importantly, such a society will be inimical to and in conflict with the goals of a consumer society. But to take note of this directs our attention to the extent to which these norms are to some extent already accepted in a variety of those settings—households, workplaces, schools, parishes—in which resistance to the goals and norms of a consumer society is recurrently generated. And, where such resistance is found, it is characteristically within groups whose social relationships are those of giving and receiving.

Thirdly, among the distinguishing marks of communities thus structured is the importance that they attach to the needs of children and the needs of the disabled. Partly this is a matter of the allocation of attention and other resources. Children are never able to constitute an interest group in the modern sense of that word. And what children need can rarely be adequately supplied only by their own families. They are therefore cared for adequately only when the care that they receive, although inevitably constrained by the limits of the community's resources, is not constrained by predictions about how much those children will one day give in return. And as it is with the care needed by children, so it is too with the care needed by the old and the mentally and physically infirm. What matters is not only that in this kind of community children and the disabled are objects of care and attention. It matters also and correspondingly that those who are no longer children recognize in children what they once were, that those who are not yet disabled by age recognize in the old what they are moving towards becoming, and that those who are not ill or injured recognize in the ill and injured what they often have been and will be and always may be. It matters also that these recognitions are not a source of fear. For such recognitions are a condition of adequate awareness of both the common needs and the common goods that are served by networks of giving and receiving and by the virtues, both of independence and of acknowledged dependence. Yet that awareness cannot itself be achieved without those same virtues.

12

Proxies, friends, truthfulness

This is of course much too brief and skeletal an account of the politics of communities of giving and receiving. But it is perhaps sufficient to provide a basis for further discussion of what I earlier suggested had to be a key role in such communities, that of someone who acts as a proxy for the radically disabled, for those who will only have a voice in the deliberations of the community, if someone else speaks for them. I had said that, if we are to be able to speak for others who are temporarily or permanently at that extremity of disablement, and so unable to speak for themselves, we can generally do so only on a basis of past friendship. What kind of friendship do I have in mind? And how in the relevant kind of friendship do I learn to speak for and on behalf of another? The perhaps surprising answer is that generally I learn this in the course of learning how to speak for myself, something more complex and more difficult than it is often taken to be.

Learning to speak for myself as an independent practical reasoner confronts, as I also noticed earlier, a number of different kinds of obstacle. Failure to reeducate my originally infantile desire to please others may result in my becoming someone whose opinions are indefinitely responsive to a pressure to conform to the opinions of certain types of other. It is not that I am not able to advance reasons, even sophisticated reasons, for holding my opinions, but that what I present as a good reason is determined by my unconscious need for approval. Or I may, because of an originally infantile resentment of my need to please others, have an equally unconscious need to be seen as not conforming to the opinions of others, a need expressed in a relentless pursuit of disagreement. In both such cases I am not a voice, but an echo. I still have to learn how to speak with my own voice. But, even if I do speak with my own voice, I may still distort my reasoning by an unconsciously selective attention to some features of my social environment at the expense of others. All attention is selective, but, if my attention is purposefully and willfully selective, so that it leads me to ignore considerations that it is important for me to entertain, my practical reasoning may be deprived of relevant premises. Or again, when I utter what I and others take to be my reasons for acting, that utterance may in fact be functioning so as to disguise some hope or fear that is motivating my action. What is it that enables us to overcome such obstacles and so to acquire the relevant moral and intellectual virtues?

It is by having our reasoning put to the question by others, by being called to account for ourselves and our actions by others, that we learn how to scrutinize ourselves as they scrutinize us and how to understand ourselves as they understand us. When others put us to the question and call us to account, it is generally in situations in which they are unclear either about just what it is that we take ourselves to be doing or about why we take it to be reasonable to act in this particular way or perhaps both. They therefore invite us to make ourselves intelligible to them, so that they may know how to respond to our actions. And what we find when we attempt to make ourselves intelligible to such questioning others is that sometimes we also need to make ourselves intelligible to ourselves. What kind of intelligibility is this?

It is not the intelligibility of performances in accordance with the requirements of roles, where although the actions are performed by individuals, most of those actions are generally understood as required of *anyone* who happens to occupy that role and are not therefore to be made intelligible by reference to the characteristics of this or that individual. The individual in the role of ticket collector, sales person, or prison guard is essentially replaceable and what we respond to is not the individual, but the role, until or unless the individual departs from the required script in some surprising and disruptive way, so that we are instead forced to confront this particular individual. How far social life is role-governed varies from culture to culture and the more that it is so governed the more likely it seems that importance will be attached to *how* individuals play their role-governed parts, so exhibiting their individuality in and through their role-playing, rather than by departing from it. But in both types of case we need to distinguish between what the individual brings to and takes from the various roles that she or he successfully occupies and the roles themselves. What each individual has is a history that is peculiarly her or his own and to invite an individual to make her or himself intelligible to us, perhaps as a preliminary to justifying her or his actions, is to invite that individual to tell us as much of that history as is needed—most often only some very small part of it, sometimes a good deal more.

When we know other people well, when we have known the same individual in a number of different roles and at different stages of her or his life, we generally do not need to ask the individual for such an account. We can already supply it ourselves. But even with people whom we know well, we are sometimes puzzled. And what we have to offer each other, if we are to be able to justify our actions to each other, is to offer at least a partial explanation of how as a practical reasoner one could have come to make the judgments about one's own good and about the common good that inform and direct one's present actions. The questions by which others call us to account may not mention either good explicitly. They are often of the form: 'What on earth did you think you were doing in doing *that?*' *or* 'How could you have possibly thought it right (or tolerable or forgivable) to treat us like *this?*' But they can always be paraphrased by such questions as: 'What good did you take yourself to be pursuing in doing *that?*' *or* 'Why did you misconceive your good or our good in *this* way?' And the only adequate answer to such questions will be either an account of the good aimed at which makes the relevant actions not only intelligible, but also justifiable *or* an account which reveals the agent's mistakes and so provides her or him with reasons for acting differently in the future.

To engage in this dialogue of question and answer, so that we make ourselves accountable to others and treat ourselves as accountable to them, we have to become able to assume the other's point of view, so that the concerns to which we respond in giving our account are the ones that are in fact genuinely theirs. If we are successful in so doing, we become able to speak with the other's voice and, if the conversation between us is sufficiently extended through time and is wide-ranging enough in its subject matter, we will become able to speak with the voice of the other systematically, that is, to assert, to question and to prescribe in the light of the other's conception of the other's individual good and the other's conception of our common good. In achieving accountability we will have learned not only how to speak to, but also how to speak for the other. We will, in the home or in the workplace or in other shared activity, have become—in one sense of that word—friends. And in so doing we will have learned how to fill the role of a proxy. In practice of course we are often very imperfect proxies for those whose disablement has deprived them of a voice of their own. But the kind of character that we have to acquire in order to be a friend or to act as a proxy, the virtues that we need for those relationships, are the same virtues that we need in general. Yet of course for these purposes some virtues are of special importance, virtues without which there could not be accountability. What are they?

We first of all and most obviously owe to others elementary truthfulness in our accounts, so that they can learn from us and we from them. When Aquinas distinguishes between lies that are mortal sins and lies that are not, he invites us to ask of any lie whether it is about something "the knowledge of which is relevant to someone's good" (S. T. IIa–IIae 110, 4). If it is, it is a mortal sin, an act of injustice that deprives the other of what we owe to her or him (IIa–IIae 109, 3). But this duty of justice to others does not exhaust what truthfulness in accountability requires. It is peculiarly important to us as well as to others that in being truthful about our actions we do not either exaggerate or diminish the part that we played in the events that we are narrating. We have to avoid the vices both of boastfulness and of self-deprecation. Boastfulness is not just a matter of our exaggerating what we did. It is also a matter of our not acknowledging the extent to which what we did depended on the contributions of others. And self-deprecation is in part a refusal to allow others to acknowledge our contributions to their achievements. Both vices focus attention on us and obscure our relationship to others. Truthfulness, it turns out, is one of the virtues of acknowledged dependence.

A first type of offense against truthfulness then consists in unjustly preventing others from learning what they need to learn, and a second type consists in concealing from view the nature of our relationships to those others. A third type of offense against truthfulness has to do with our relationship to the shared language in which we speak with others, when making ourselves accountable to them. This type of offense, following Richard Rorty's usage, I shall name "irony." Rorty has called the "set of words" which human beings "employ to justify their actions, their beliefs and their lives" their "final vocabulary" (*Contingency, Irony and Solidarity*, Cambridge: Cambridge University Press, 1989, p. 73) and has commended those whom he calls ironists, those whose attitude towards their own final vocabulary is one of "radical and continuing doubts," because they are aware of other alternative final vocabularies and also believe that there are no rational criteria by appeal to which a choice between vocabularies might be justified. Rorty speaks of the ironists' "realization that anything can be made to look good or bad by being redescribed" and he says of ironists that they are "never quite able to take themselves seriously because . . . always aware of the contingency and fragility of their final vocabularies, and thus of their selves" (pp. 73–74).

Why do I take irony thus characterized to be an offense against the kind of truthfulness in accountability that is required by the virtues of acknowledged dependence? A first consideration to note is that the vocabulary in which I make intelligible and justify or fail to justify my actions, beliefs, and life within a network of relationships of giving and receiving is never merely *mine*. It is always *ours*, a set of shared expressions put to shared uses, uses embedded in a wide range of common practices of receiving and giving, in a common form of life. When I am called to account as a practical reasoner in this shared evaluative language, what I am invited to consider is whether what is said about me is or is not true and justified in the light of our shared standards of truth and justification. I fail in responding to this invitation, not only if I were to lie, but also if I were to become evasive, if, for example, in such a context I were to remark that "anything can be made to look good or bad by being redescribed." For in the shared vocabulary of the common life of such a society, I may only justly claim that my action should be redescribed, by showing that it has been in some relevant respect misdescribed. If it is suggested to me, for example, that I have been thoughtless and irresponsible in not considering any but the most immediate effects on others of certain of my actions, I might perhaps rebut this accusation by showing that, given the information made available to me, I could scarcely have acted otherwise, or by showing that only the short-term effects of those particular actions were my responsibility and that someone else was responsible for the long-term effects. But what I may not do, except at the cost of further evasion, is to regard or to invite others to regard those actions through which I discharge or fail to discharge my responsibilities with ironic detachment.

Ironic detachment involves a withdrawal from our common language and our shared judgments and thereby from the social relationships which presuppose the use of that language in making those judgments. But it is in and through those relationships, as I remarked earlier, that we acquire and sustain not only our knowledge of others, but also that self-knowledge which depends on the confirmatory judgments of others. So, if my ironic detachment is genuine and not mere pretense, it involves me in putting in question not only my communal allegiances, but even what I have taken to be my self-knowledge. I am to find a vantage point quite outside those relationships and commitments that have made me what I now am. But what might this be?

On this Rorty might well comment: that what he praised is an ironic attitude towards one's own final vocabulary, but not an ironic attitude towards those commitments, those solidarities, which are the basis for the trust that others may repose in us. And Rorty's trenchant and admirable expression of his own social democratic commitments and solidarities does not seem to be in the least ironic. So over what then do we disagree? Presumably over whether it is or is not in the end possible to separate one's attitude towards the vocabulary through which one's commitments and solidarities are articulated from one's attitude towards those commitments and solidarities.

Attempts to answer this question have a long history. Hegel's answer to it was the basis for his criticism of Friedrich Schlegel's defense of irony (*Vorlesungen über die Ästhetik* I, 95). And the retort to critics of either Schlegel's or Rorty's conception of irony will always be that only irony enables us to adopt an adequately critical attitude towards our own evaluative vocabularies. After all, when Rorty introduced his account of the ironist, his purpose was to stress the importance of cultivating an awareness of alternative final vocabularies in order to undermine too easy an acceptance of our own. So my claim that from the standpoint of the virtues this type of irony is a species of moral evasion may seem to imply an unwarranted and too uncritical attitude towards my own final vocabulary. Does it?

It implies at the very least a tension between the view that I have taken of evaluative commitments and skeptical questioning. If and insofar as it is necessary, in order to take up an adequately critical attitude, to disengage ourselves from our relationships and commitments and to view them with a cold and sceptical eye, then at that point we will have distanced ourselves from our commitments in a way that may always endanger those commitments. It follows that, even if there is a time for criticism, there are also times when criticism has to be put aside and to negotiate the relationship between these successfully itself requires the exercise of the virtues and a further recognition of our need for the virtues. But neither time is a time for irony.

Yet it does appear that by saying this I have already foreclosed on certain possibilities of criticism. For if the negotiation of the relationship of criticism to commitment itself requires a continuing recognition of the need for the virtues, both those of independence and those of acknowledged dependence, then I am surely precluded, at least at the level of practice, from putting the relevant set of virtues seriously in question. And this is to say that I have excluded the possibility of genuinely radical criticism. Such criticism, it will be said, is made possible only by stepping outside the circle, by discarding, either in imagination or in actuality, that in me which is committed to that particular set of virtues and so separating myself from the common life of those relationships in which I am accountable to others. Only by so doing can I find a standpoint that is sufficiently external to the evaluative attitudes and practices that are to be put to the question. Insofar as I remain entangled within the relationships and commitments of giving and receiving, I am no more than a prisoner of shared prejudices. What reply, if any, can be made to this accusation?

13

Moral commitment and rational enquiry

It can only be answered by taking my overall argument one step further. That argument, it may be opportune to recall, has proceeded through the following stages. It began from two distinct, although related, starting points. The first was a consideration of what it is in and from our animal nature that we share with members of other intelligent, but non-language-using species, such as dolphins, a consideration designed to show not only that we are right to ascribe to members of at least some of those species intentions and reasons for action, but also that in our own beginnings as rational agents we are very close to their condition and that our identity was then and remains an animal identity. The second was an emphasis upon the vulnerability and disability that pervade human life, in early childhood, in old age and during those periods when we are injured or physically or mentally ill, and the extent of our consequent dependence on others.

From those starting points I attempted to answer the question of what it would be for thus vulnerable and dependent rational animals to flourish and what qualities of character we would need, if we were to be able to receive from others what we need them to give to us and to give to others what we need to receive from them. The answer that I have sketched is that in order to flourish, we need both those virtues that enable us to function as independent and accountable practical reasoners and those virtues that enable us to acknowledge the nature and extent of our dependence on others. Both the acquisition and the exercise of those virtues are possible only insofar as we participate in social relationships of giving and receiving, social relationships governed by and partially defined by the norms of the natural law.

Finally I have asked what social and political forms are required to achieve the common good of those who participate in the relevant kinds of relationship of giving and receiving. And it has emerged that both the moral and political relationships that are required for the achievement of that common good involve commitments that are in some respects unconditional not only to a certain range of goods, but also to those particular others together with whom we attempt to achieve that common good. Those commitments seem to preclude us from putting seriously in question that practical understanding of goods, virtues, rules, and relationships which is presupposed by our commitments and which we share with many of those same others. For to assume the standpoint of the serious questioner seems to involve standing aside from, separating ourselves from, prior commitments. But is this in fact so? Can we perhaps give a rationally defensible account of the relationship of moral commitment to critical rational enquiry that enables us to identify and to satisfy the legitimate demands of both? A first step towards supplying such an account has been taken, when we understand that critical rational enquiry is not itself the kind of activity that anyone can undertake on her or his own. For the same reasons that I cited, when I argued that we are able to become and to continue as practical reasoners only in and through our relationships to others, we are able to engage in critical enquiry about our beliefs, conceptions, and presuppositions only in and through relationships to others. Rational enquiry is essentially social and, like other types of social activity, it is directed towards its own specific goals, it depends for its success on the virtues of those who engage in it, and it requires relationships and evaluative commitments of a particular kind.

Rational enquiry about my practical beliefs, relationships, and commitments is therefore not something that *I* undertake by attempting to separate myself from the whole set of my beliefs, relationships, and commitments and to view them from some external standpoint. It is something that *we* undertake from within *our* shared mode of practice by asking, when we have good reason to do so, what the strongest and soundest objections are to this or that particular belief or concept that we have up to this point taken for granted. Such rational enquiry extends and amplifies our everyday practical reasoning. For when I take myself to have good reasons for acting in this way rather than that, I or someone else may always find good reasons to raise the question of whether what I take to be good reasons really are good reasons. And it may turn out to be impossible to answer this question without examining the standard to which we have hitherto implicitly appealed in evaluating reasons as better or worse. The further questions of what authority these standards have and why may then arise, so that we find ourselves compelled to raise philosophical issues in order to find rationally compelling grounds for deciding to act in one way rather than another.

Such enquiries may provide us with grounds for the criticism, revision, or even rejection of many of our judgments, our standards of judgment, our relationships and our institutions. And the best rational defense of our present judgments, standards, relationships, and institutions is that, after undergoing such critical scrutiny, they have proved able to withstand the strongest objections that have so far been advanced against them. When some local community embodying networks of giving and receiving is in good order, it is generally and characteristically because its judgments, standards, relationships, and institutions have been periodically the subject of communal debate and enquiry and have taken their present form in part as a result of such debate and enquiry.

Yet it would be a mistake, a moral as well as philosophical mistake, to infer that anything whatever can be reasonably and justly put in question. What we take to be a good reason for action in a particular situation in key part depends, so I have contended, upon how far we have acquired or failed to acquire the virtues relevant to that situation. And what on this or that type of occasion we take to be a good reason for asking for a justification of the reasons for which we or others are acting or proposing to act is likewise a matter of our moral character, our virtues and vices. Consider a situation in which someone who comes across a seriously injured or ill or starving stranger, has the resources to provide needed help, and no one else both willing and able to do so is at hand. The stranger's urgent need provides a sufficient reason for going to her or his aid. Suppose now that a bystander, unwilling her- or himself to give help, asks for a justification of the judgment that the stranger's need provides a sufficient reason for going to her or his aid. It is one of the marks of the virtues of just generosity that those who possess it are not only disposed to find in someone's need in such circumstances a sufficient reason for going to her or his aid, but will also be unable to conceive of such a reason as requiring or being open to further justification. To offer or even to request such a justification is itself a sign of defective virtue.

This at first sight must seem to be incompatible with what was said earlier about the structure of practical reasoning. For I have represented that structure as deductive. It is because the human good is what it is that in order to achieve it we need to acquire the virtues. And it is because the virtues are what they are that we need on this or that occasion to judge and to act in this or that way. So when we have progressed far enough in the moral life to have embodied in our practice a directedness towards some more or less adequate conception of the human good and to have transformed our inclinations and passions so that we have acquired something more than the rudiments of the virtues, we will on occasion be able to represent what it is that makes it rational for us to act as we do by constructing a chain of reasoning whose first premises concern the human good, whose intermediate steps specify what the virtues require, if the human good is to be achieved, and whose conclusion is the action that it is good and best for us to perform here and now.

Hence it may seem that a radical justification for my action will always be of the form: 'Because so to act will contribute to my achievement of my good, *qua* human being'. It follows that if, in the type of example that I have outlined, I do what the virtue of just generosity requires and act so as to aid the stranger in need, my reason for action, if it is a good reason, will never be simply that the stranger was in urgent need, but must also be that by acting so as to meet that need I contributed to the achievement of my own good. There is then after all a further justification for aiding the stranger. But this objection rests on a mistake.

What a virtue such as that of just generosity requires of me is that in situations where the responsibility to meet gross and urgent need falls upon me I find in that gross and urgent need sufficient reason to act and neither ask nor look for any further reason. I do indeed have good reason for becoming and acting as someone whose character is informed by the virtue of just generosity. Without that virtue I cannot achieve my good. But insofar as I have in fact acquired that virtue—it, like other virtues, can be acquired to varying degrees—I will have learned to act without thought of any justification beyond the need of those given into my care.

So there can be a chain of sound justificatory reasoning that runs from the nature of the human good to the need for each of the virtues, and from what the virtues require to answers to the question of what action should be performed in these particular circumstances by me here and now. And the soundness or otherwise of that chain of reasoning is what makes it practically rational or irrational to act in this way or that. But to act as reason requires may on occasion exclude any reference by the agent her- or himself to that chain of reasoning. So it is with our response to gross and urgent need in those cases where we bear the responsibility for meeting it. And concerning such cases not to allow even the shadow of a doubt about what we ought to do and why is one of the touchstones of character.

It is of great importance not to confuse character of this kind, character informed by the virtue of just generosity, with altruism, as it is usually understood. A presupposition for the application of the notion of altruism is a conception of human beings as divided in their inclinations and passions, some of those being self-regarding, others being other-regarding. Altruists are those in whom on occasion at least the other-regarding inclinations and passions prevail over the self-regarding. The altruist is the counterpart to the egoist and there are of course influential accounts of altruism according to which it is either a disguised form of egoism or, in some more sophisticated versions, a transformation of egoism in the interests of satisfying egoism's original goals.

We do indeed as infants, as children, and even as adolescents, experience sharp conflicts between egoistic and altruistic impulses and desires. But the task of education is to transform and integrate those into an inclination towards both the common good and our individual goods, so that we become neither self-rather-than-other-regarding nor other-rather-than-self-regarding, neither egoists nor altruists, but those whose passions and inclinations are directed to what is both our good and the good of others. Self-sacrifice, it follows, is as much of vice, as much of a sign of inadequate moral development, as selfishness.

How the virtues enable us to view ourselves and others and our relationship to others, as actual or potential members of some network of giving and receiving, is perhaps best captured by Aristotle's discussion in Book IX of the *Nicomachean Ethics* (1166a 1–1166b 29), where he argues that, insofar as we are good, we stand to ourselves, just as we stand to our friends, and vice versa. It matters, of course, and this Aristotle does not say, that my love for each of my friends has to be a love for that friend as characterized by her or his particularity, by what makes her or him a distinctive human being with her or his own peculiar abilities and resources for giving and her or his own peculiar needs and dependencies. It is what is distinctive in the character, resources, and circumstances of each, and correspondingly what is distinctive in my character, resources, and circumstances that gives me reason to act in this way towards this friend, in another way towards that. It is in and through the relationships of friends that the particularity of each and the distinctive value of each as being *this* particular individual with her or his own distinctive good to achieve is accorded recognition. And we each of us need this recognition, if we are to pursue our own good effectively within networks of giving and receiving. It is not only for the achievement of our common good that we are dependent on the other members of our communities, but we depend too on some particular others to achieve most of our individual goods. It follows that when we reflect together critically upon our shared practically effective beliefs and concepts it must be in such a way as not to threaten this mutual recognition. For it is only on the basis of this recognition that we can ensure that our deliberations really are the deliberations of the community, rather than an adversarial exercise of dialectical skill by individuals with opposing views, in which the outcome of the argument may be to undermine someone's standing as a member of the community or even the whole notion of mutual recognition. Here too there is a limitation placed on rational criticism and enquiry.

Yet the relationship between moral commitment and rational criticism and enquiry is not only or primarily a matter of the one imposing limitations and constraints upon the other. It is only because and when a certain range of moral commitments is shared, as it must be within a community structured by networks of giving and receiving, that not only shared deliberation, but shared critical enquiry concerning that deliberation and the way of life of which it is a part, becomes possible. Truthfulness about their shared practical experience, justice in respect of the opportunity that each participant receives to advance her or his arguments, and an openness to refutation are all prerequisites of critical enquiry. And it is only insofar as we all of us treat those virtues as constitutive of our common good, and ascribe to the standards that they require of us an authority that is independent of the interests and desires of each of us, that we will be able to engage in genuinely critical enquiry. Moral commitment to these virtues and to the common good is not an external constraint upon, but a condition of enquiry and criticism.

It follows that someone who was able and willing at some point in her or his life to separate her or himself, in practice as well as in theory, wholly and not only in part, not in this or that stage or aspect of her or his life, but in all her or his activities and in all her or his sufferings, from those social relationships that are informed by the norms of giving and receiving, and from the virtues that sustain those relationships, including that of just generosity towards and gratitude to the able and the disabled alike, would by rejecting all the relevant moral commitments have also cut her or himself off from participation in any common work of rational enquiry and criticism. That this is indeed so would perhaps have been no more than an inference, were it not for Nietzsche's heroic work and life.

I call that work and life heroic, because by any standard Nietzsche had to exhibit quite extraordinary courage to live as he did and to write as he did. That others did not possess the same courage he was all too scornfully aware. And it was precisely of lack of such courage that he accused those who remained, as he saw it, imprisoned by the morality of the illusions that they are accountable to others and that their responsiveness to the sufferings of others is for anyone's good. So Nietzsche in a heroic series of acts isolated himself by ridding himself, so far as is humanly possible, of the commitments required by the virtues of acknowledged dependence. He was then able to tell us from that new vantage point how human nature and the human condition appear from it. And the account that he provided, item by item, stands in the starkest of oppositions to and is an inversion of the account presupposed by the practice of the virtues of acknowledged dependence.

Both accounts begin from a consideration of our animal

nature. But it is not, as with Aristotle and Aquinas, the relationship of human reason to the *phronesis* of other intelligent species that interests Nietzsche. It is instead the contrast between the animal as predator and the domesticated animal. "It is not the ferocity of the beast of prey that requires a moral disguise but the herd animal with its profound mediocrity, timidity, and boredom with itself" (*The Gay Science* V, 352, trans. W. Kaufman, New York: Random House, 1974). The human animal is indeed liable to sickness. But pity, which is the response of the human herd animal, is itself one more debilitating form of sickness. Pity "preserves what is ripe for destruction; it defends life's disinherited and condemned; through the abundance of the ill-constituted of all kinds which it *retains* in life it gives life itself a gloomy and questionable aspect" (*The Antichrist* 7, trans. R. J. Hollingdale, London: Penguin Books, 1968).

It is not that, on Nietzsche's view, *my* sickness may not be valuable to *me*. Life can be merciful in providing this "hard schooling": "sickness for years perhaps, that demands the most extreme strength of will and self-sufficiency" (*The Will to Power*, 912, trans. W. Kaufman, London: Weidenfeld and Nicolson, 1967). And what I will have learned, if I have become strong, is that I am accountable only to me. "Can you furnish yourself with your own good and evil and hang up your own will alone yourself as a law?" asks Zarathustra (*Thus Spake Zarathustra* I, 'Of the Way of the Creator', trans. R. J. Hollingdale, London: Penguin Books, 1961). "Can you be judge of yourself and avenger of your law? It is terrible to be alone with the judge and avenger of your law."

Nietzsche's claim is that to be able consistently to avoid the bonds of obligations that do not arise from one's own voluntary willing is much more difficult than might be supposed. It requires a hardness and a steeling ('Of Old and New Law Tables', 29) that are the antitheses of pity. Pity is to be extinguished, for it leads to losing one's own way (*The Gay Science*, 338). And what matters most is that one's way should be one's own. Zarathustra asks: " 'This—is now *my* way: where is yours?' Thus I answered those who asked me 'the way'. For *the* way—does not exist" (*Thus Spake Zarathustra* III, 'Of the Spirit of Gravity', 2). So Nietzsche provides an alternative and rival account of what independence is, one according to which a right understanding of the virtues of independence excludes the possibility of there being any genuine virtues of acknowledged dependence.

Unsurprisingly the same radical difference appears in the contrast between the way in which friendship is understood in the two rival accounts of the virtues. From the standpoint of the virtues of acknowledged dependence, as we have already seen, we need friendships in which each goes to the aid of the other, friendships that endure over time, in peace and war, at work and at leisure, in health and in pain, sickness and disability. We are able to draw upon Aristotelianism to characterize the kind of friendship that we need, but we need more than Aristotle himself provides, because of Aristotle's reluctance to admit the extent to which our need for friendship is bound up with the sharing of our vulnerability and our wounds. (I remarked at the very beginning of this book upon how, when Aristotle discussed the particular need that we have for friends in times of adversity and loss, he insisted that only men who are unmanly are willing to have others saddened by their grief. Such men, he thought, behave as women do. Those who are manly prefer not to inflict their loss upon others by sharing it with them [*Nicomachean Ethics* IX 1171b 6–12]. Yet what we should by now have learned from the virtues of acknowledged dependence is that this is a respect in which men need to become more like women.)

Nietzsche's account of friendship goes well beyond this reluctance in its exclusion of the possibility of friendship based on mutual need. To a remarkable extent Nietzsche offers us an inverted mirror-image of the friendship required by the virtues of acknowledged dependence. "In your friend you should possess your best enemy. Your heart should feel closest to him when you oppose him" (*Thus Spake Zarathustra* I, 'Of the Friend'). And Nietzsche concluded Zarathustra's discourse on friendship by a declaration that "Woman is not yet capable of friendship." Nietzsche thus confronts us with a radical alternative way of thinking about dependence and independence in human relationships. By so doing he shows with unflinching clarity what a systematic and consistent repudiation of the virtues of acknowledged dependence involves. And in so doing he sometimes teaches us truths about those virtues that we might otherwise fail to learn. Yet, although we can learn from Nietzsche, we cannot learn from him as one who is able to participate with us in rational conversation, criticism, and enquiry. Why not?

It is because, as Nietzsche's account has made clear, among the commitments and relationships that Nietzsche had had to reject in order to escape from what he took to be their imprisoning power are just those without which shared communal deliberation cannot take place. For on Nietzsche's view when I provide what I take to be a reason for arriving at this conclusion rather than that, whether practically or theoretically, I do not appeal to a standard of justification that is independent of my own desires and drives, as in the standard of the common good, but I give expression, whether I know it or not, to whatever form the will to power may have taken in those desires and drives and I seek to overcome that which stands in the way of their expression. In place of shared enquiry there is a set of often disguised adversarial relationships. If I am to lay bare the character of those relationships, I cannot do so by means of any type of utterance that presupposes that I and those whom I address share some common good. I may prophesy to them through the mask of Zarathustra, I may propose to them a genealogical understanding of their errors, I may deploy aphorisms or arguments to dissolve their certainties or I may instead cast doubt on logic itself and therefore on argument, but in so doing I cannot but speak with the voice of an outsider, of an external commentator.

So correspondingly we cannot reply to Nietzsche on his own terms. And that we cannot is itself instructive, reminding us of how much is involved in allegiance to a conception of the common good that requires both the virtues of the independent practical reasoner and the virtues of acknowledged dependence. For this is a good common to the very young and to the very old, as well as to mature adults, to the paraplegic and to the mentally backward as well as to the athlete and to those engaged in intellectual enquiry, a good that has regard to every vulnerability to which our animal identity and our animal nature, as well as our specifically human condition expose us. It is because and insofar as rational enquiry serves and partly constitutes that common good that it is itself the good that it is.

Index